LET YOUR PEN RUN. IMAGINE FANTASTIC WORLDS

Free your mind and relax your body. Outline the shapes as you wish and let yourself be inspired by the colors and patterns of the compositions on these pages.

VOL.1/POLYCHROMIC RHAPSODY

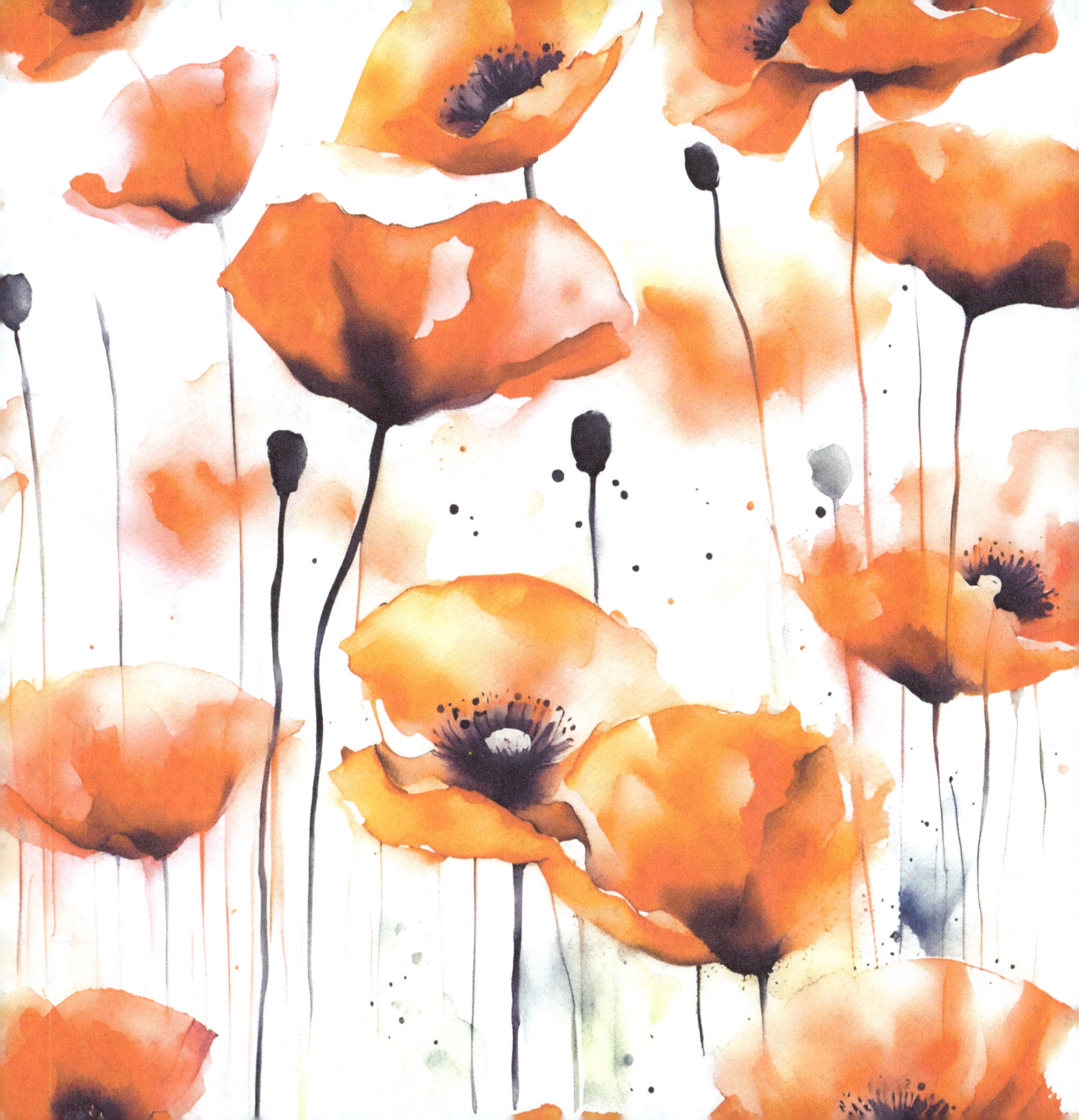

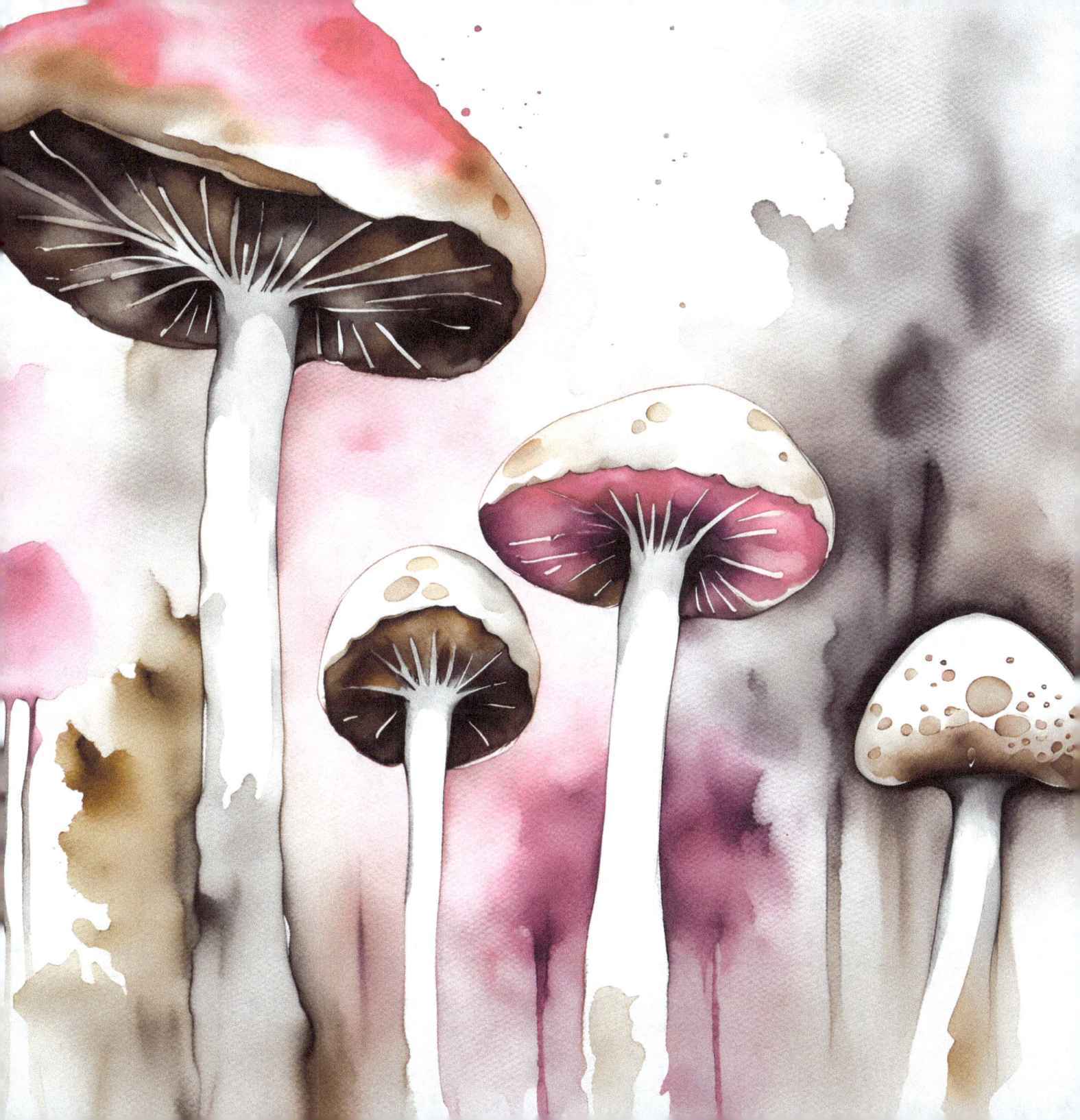

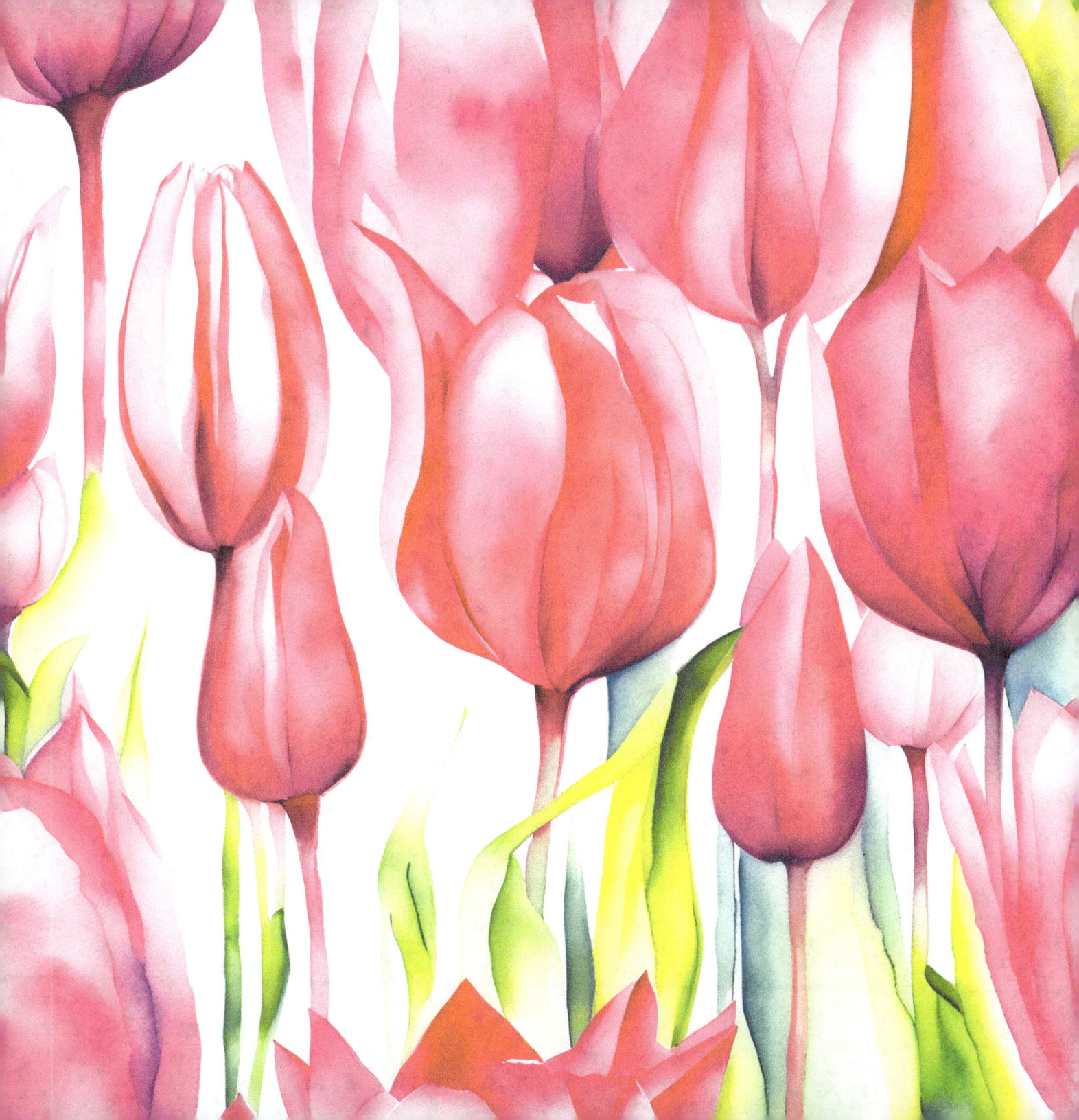

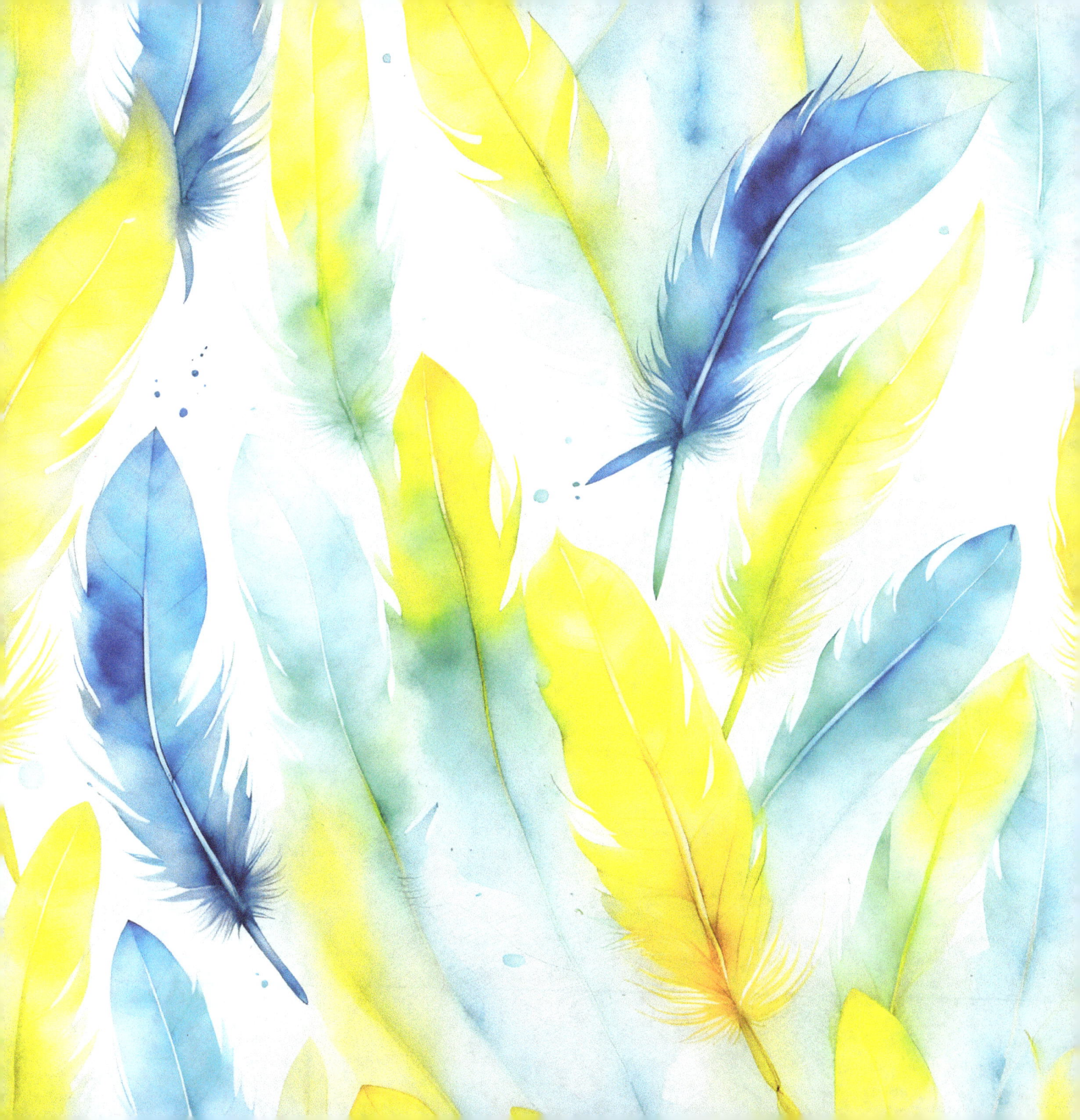

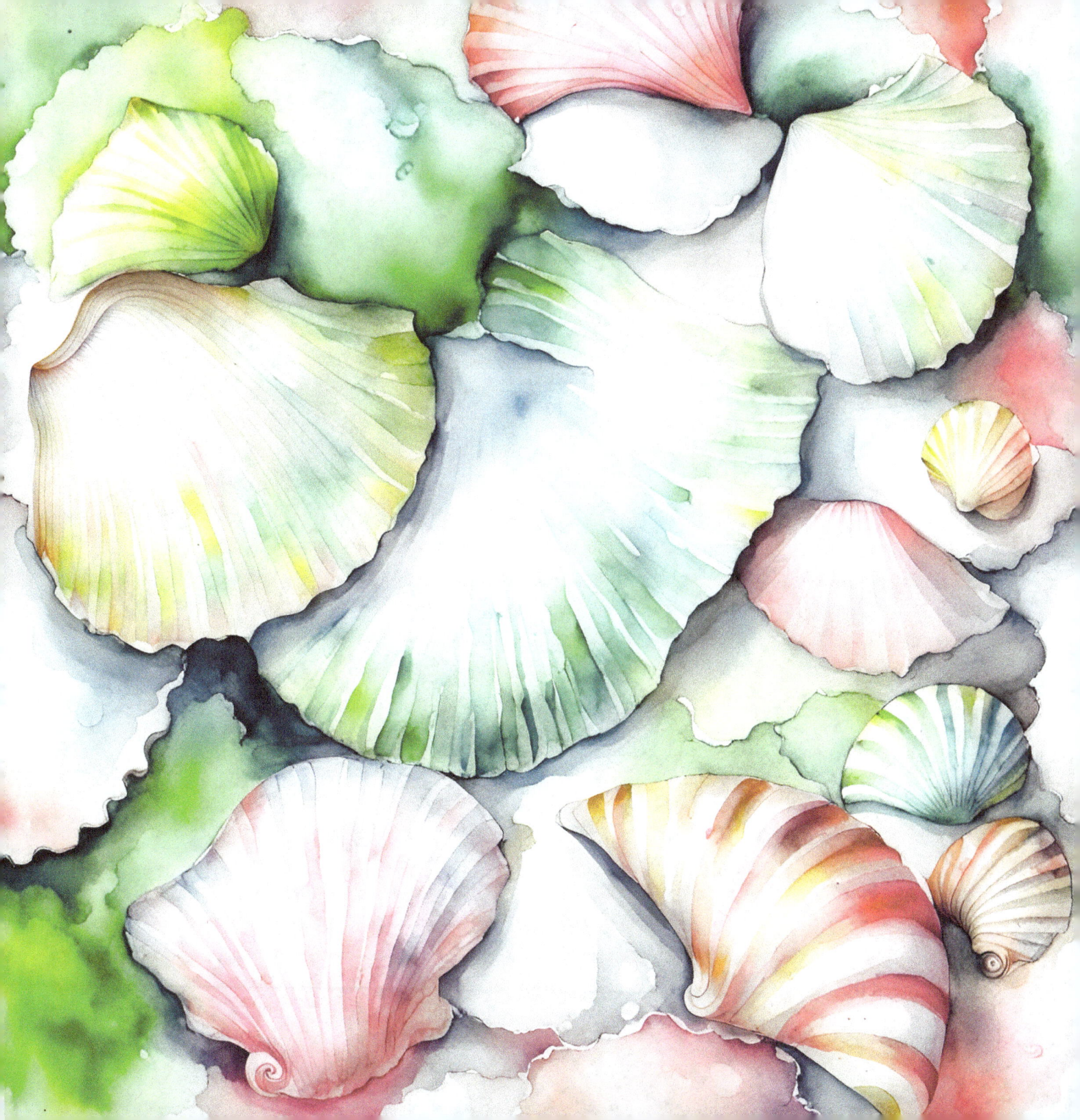

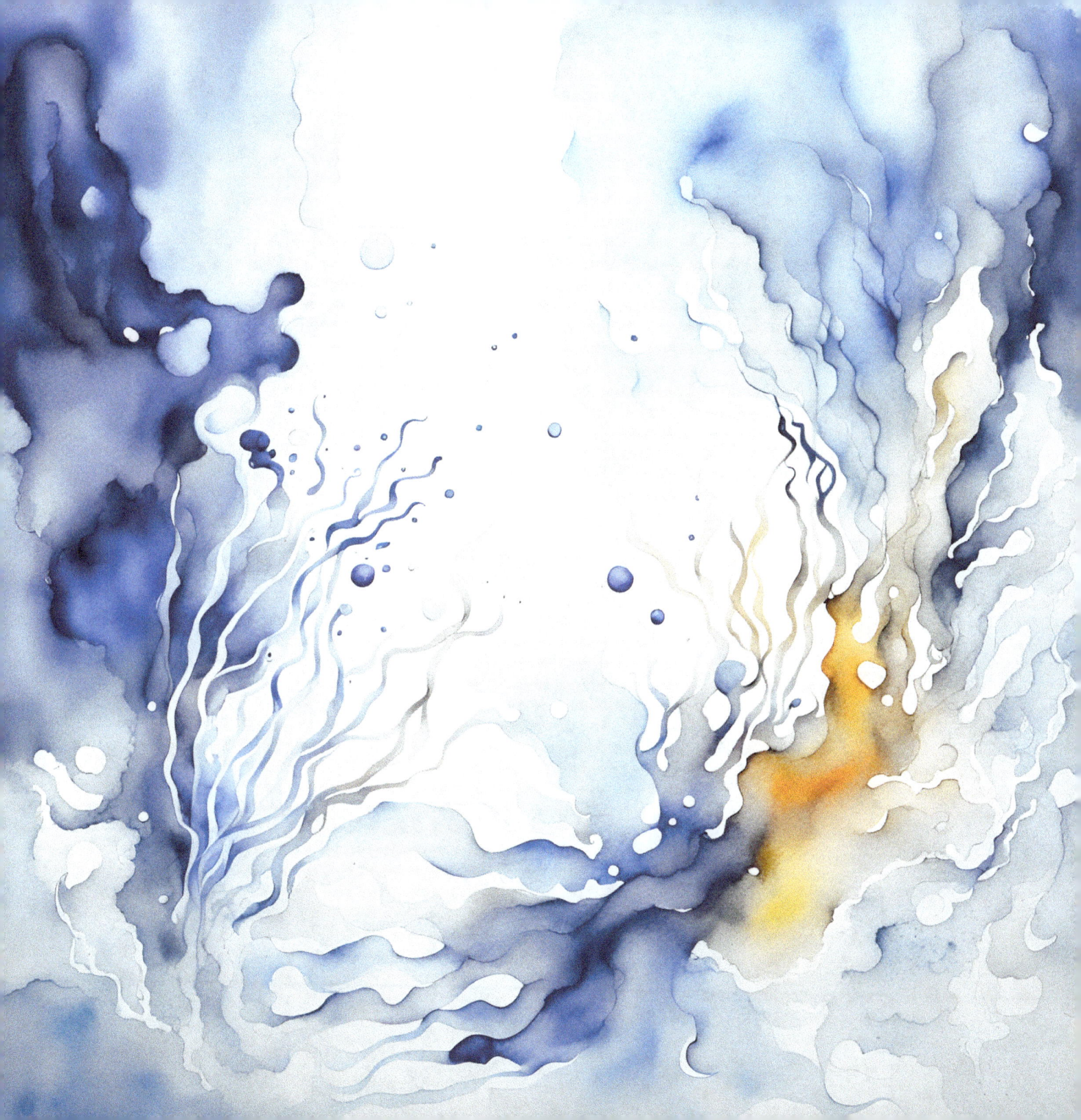

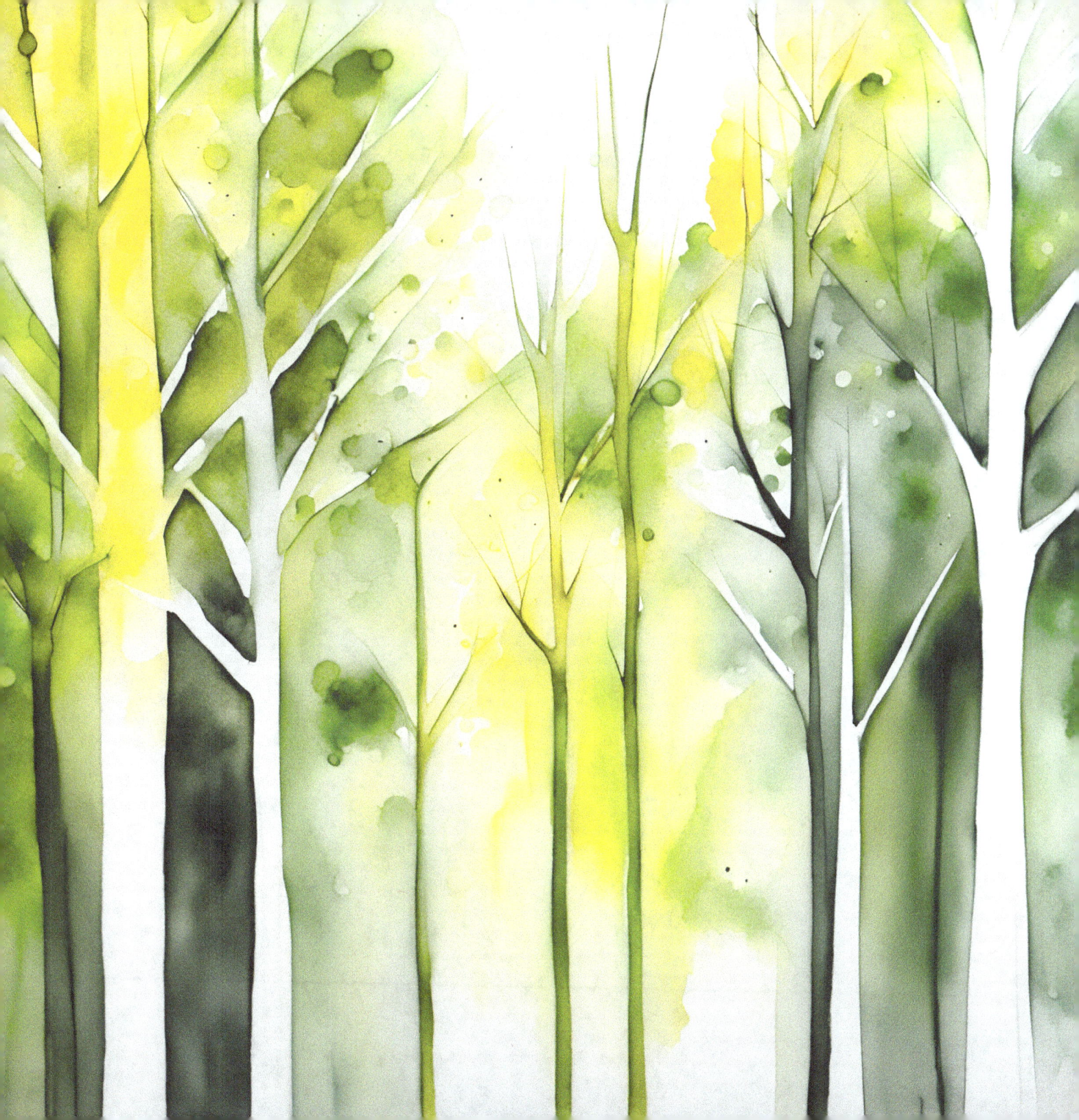

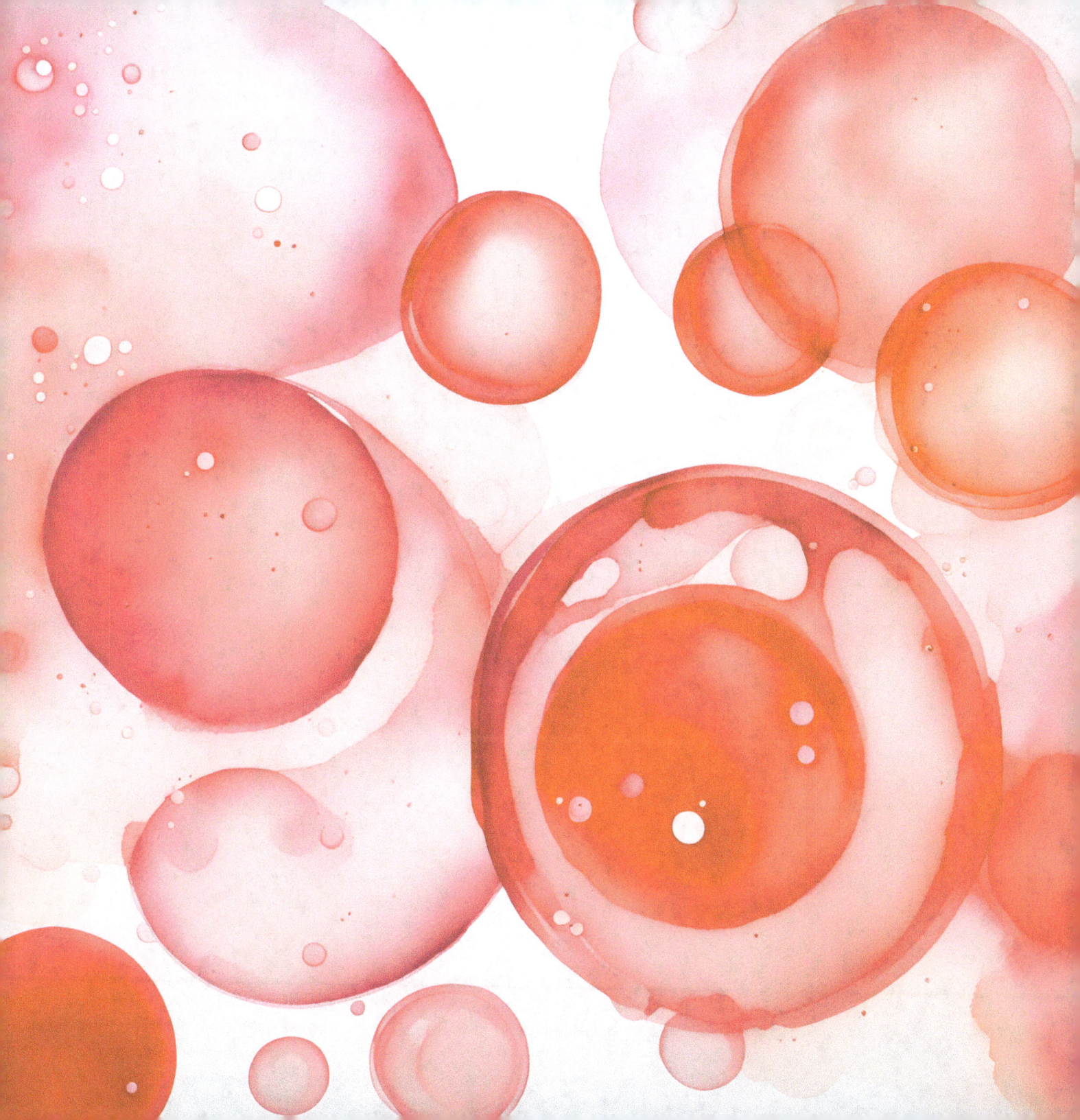

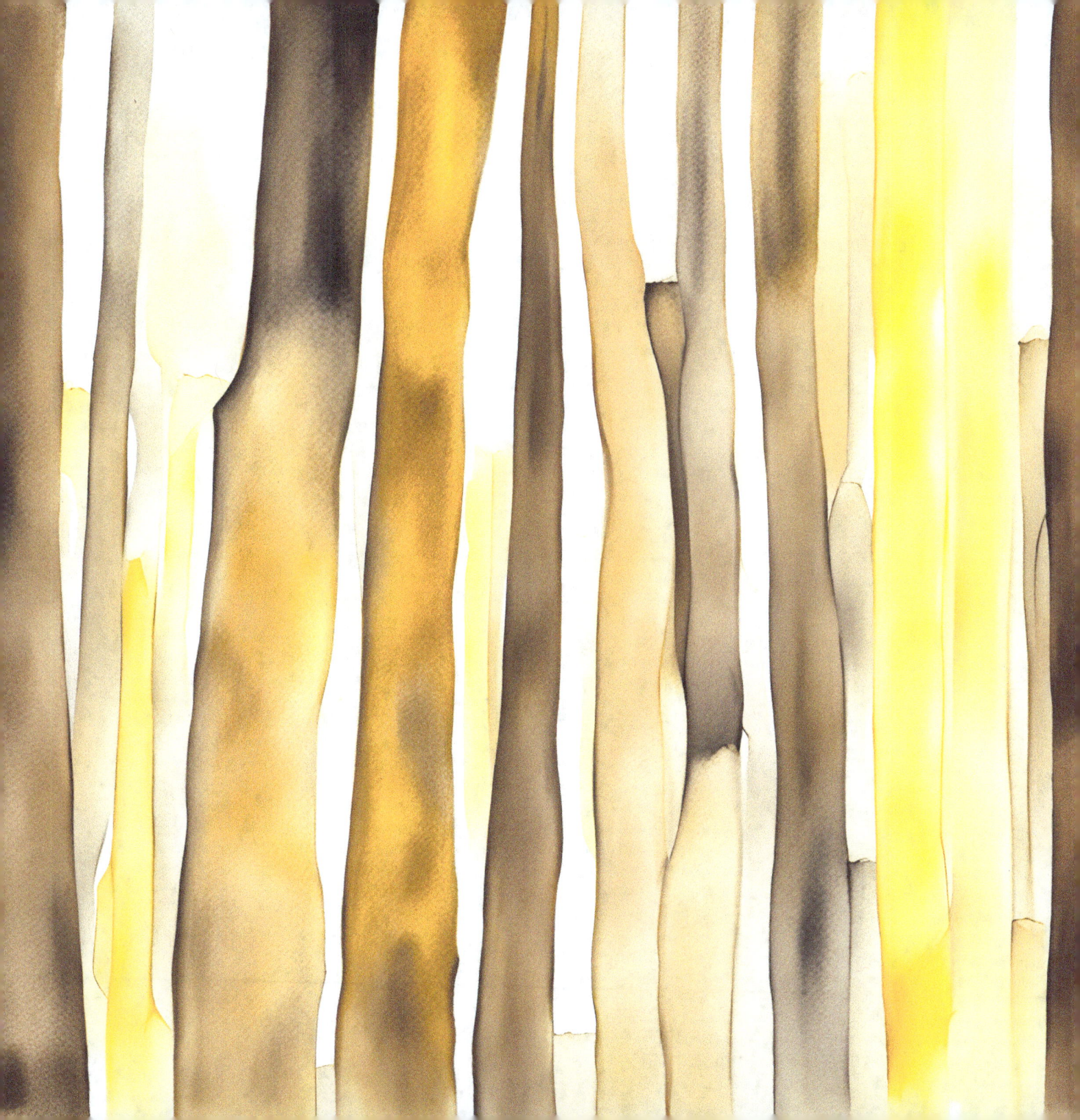

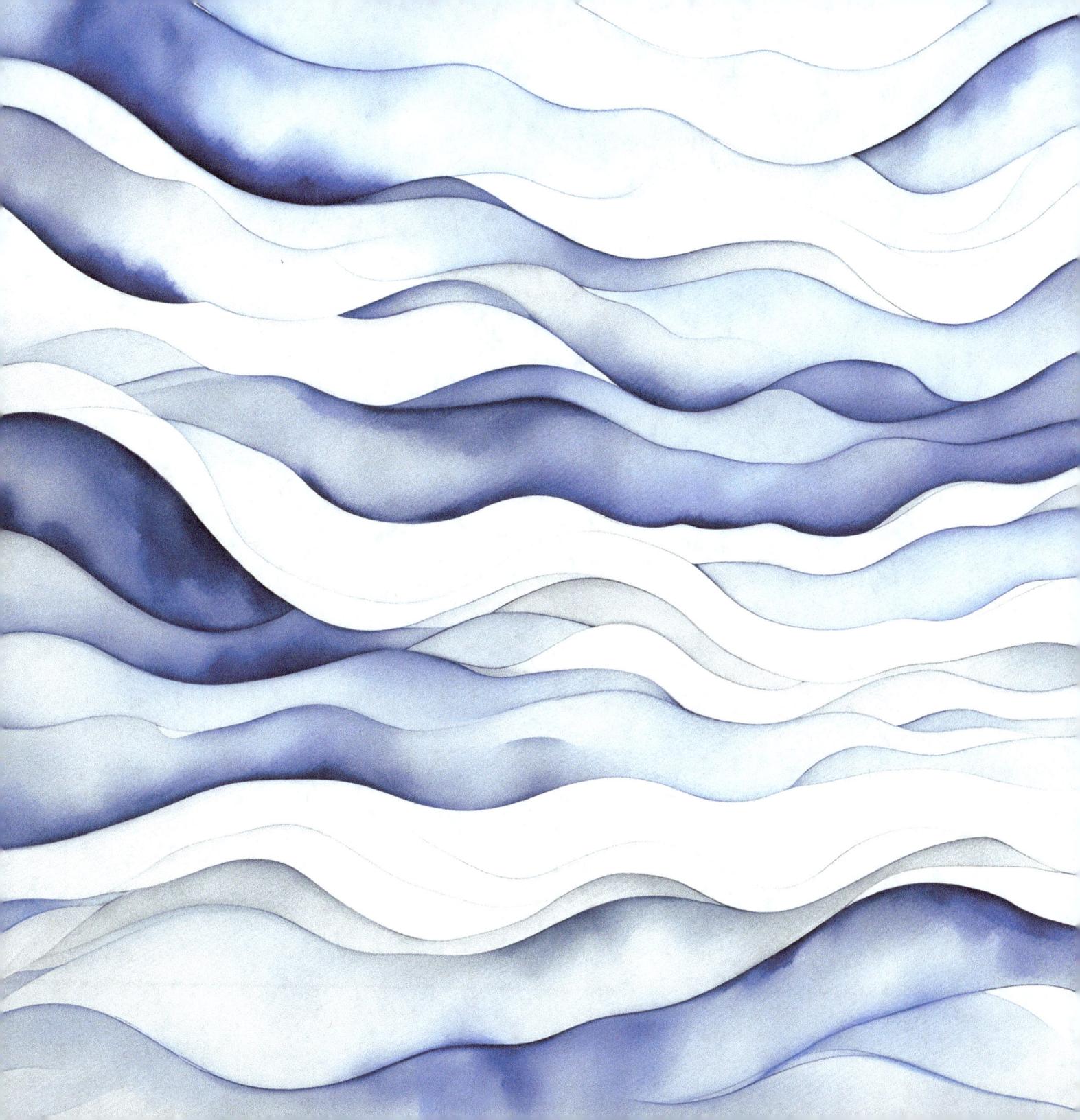

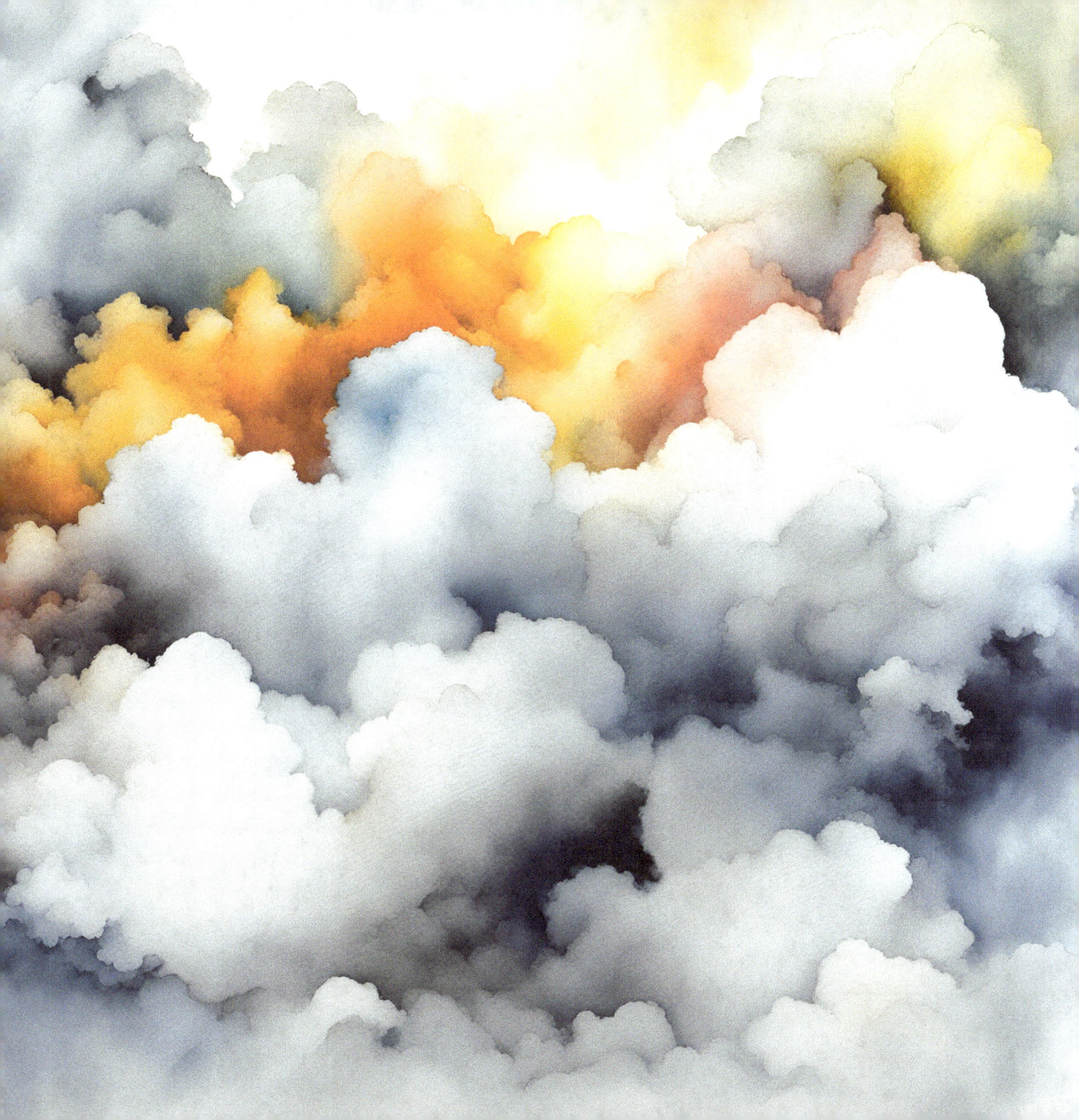

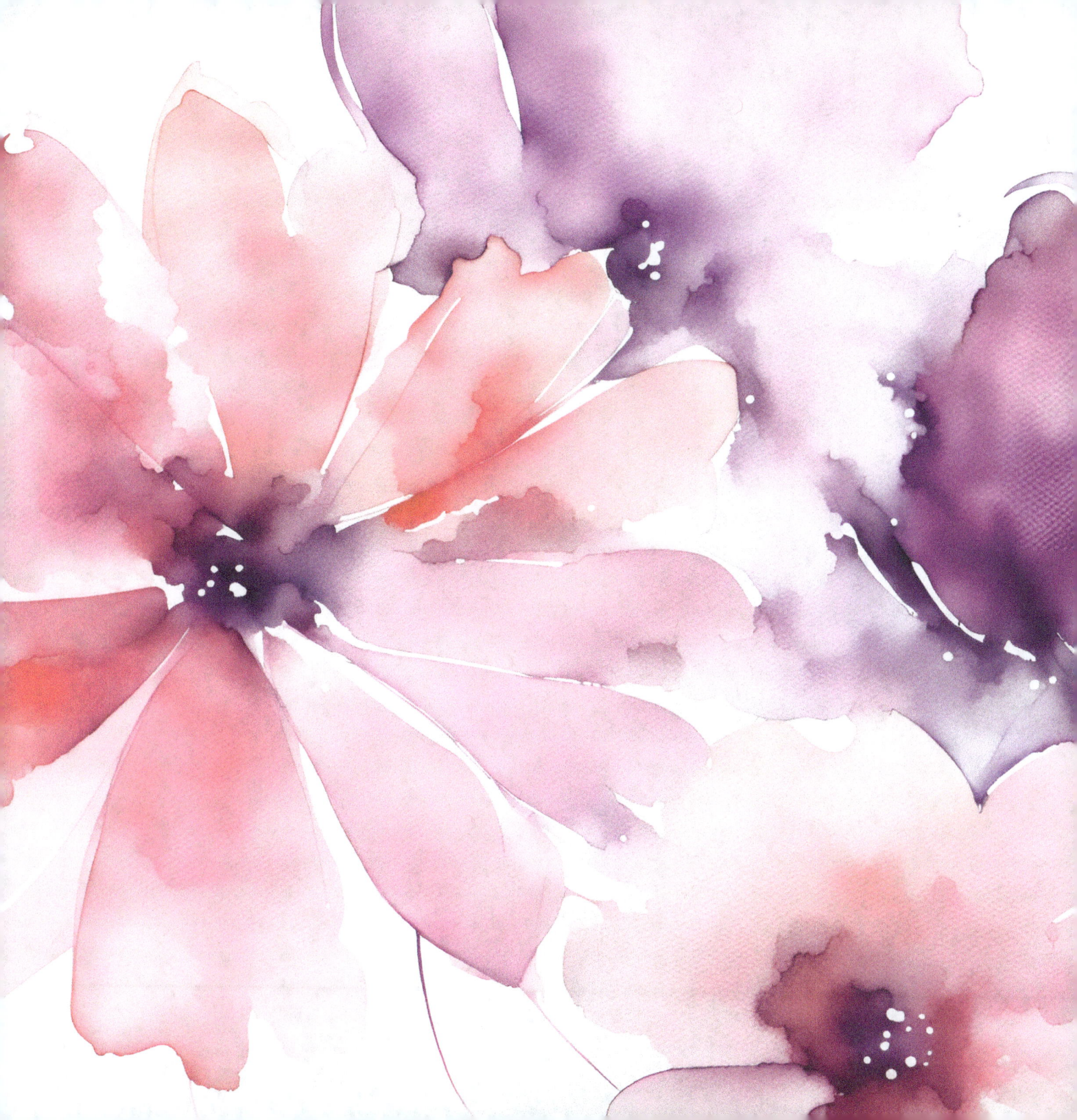

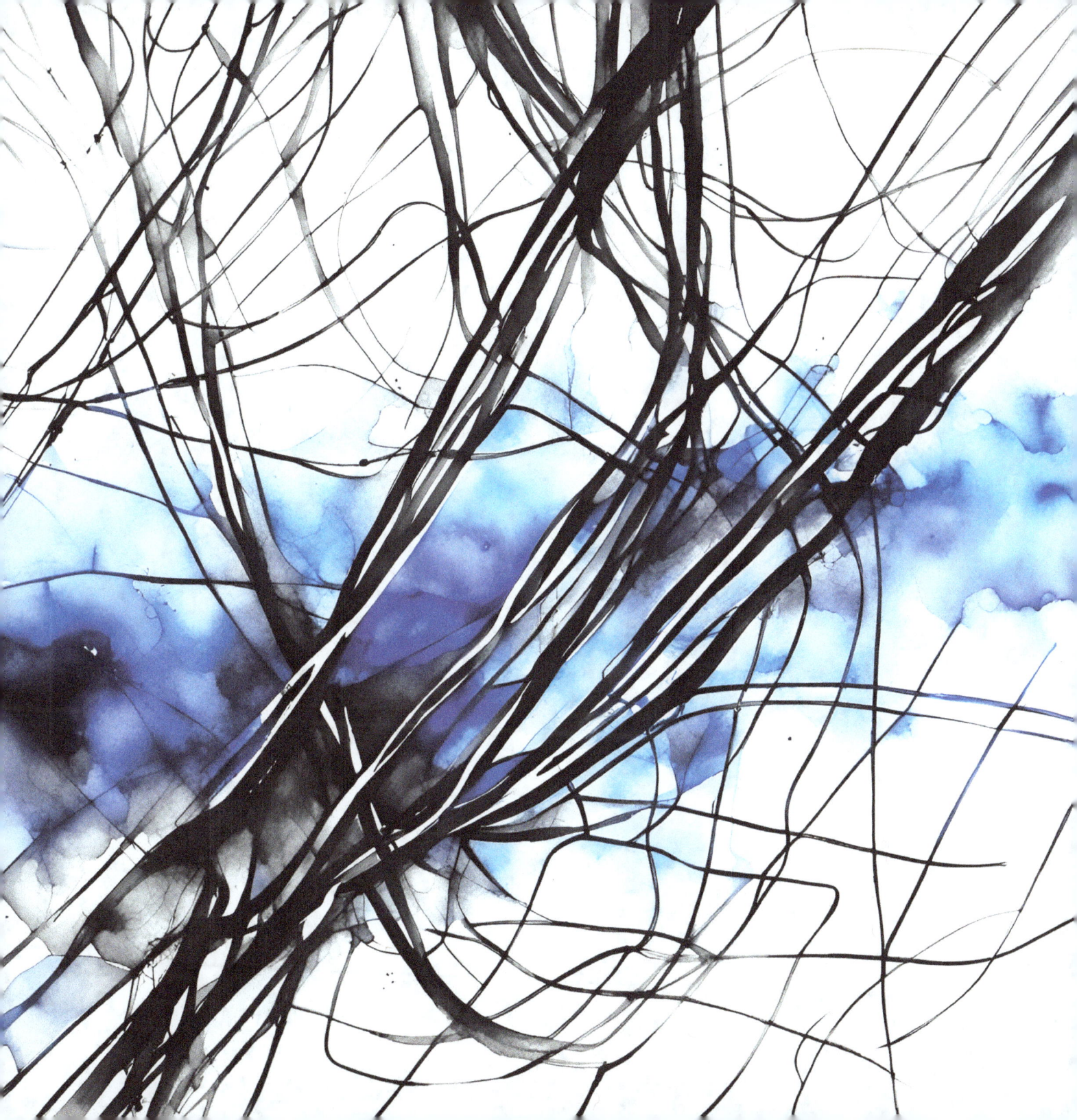

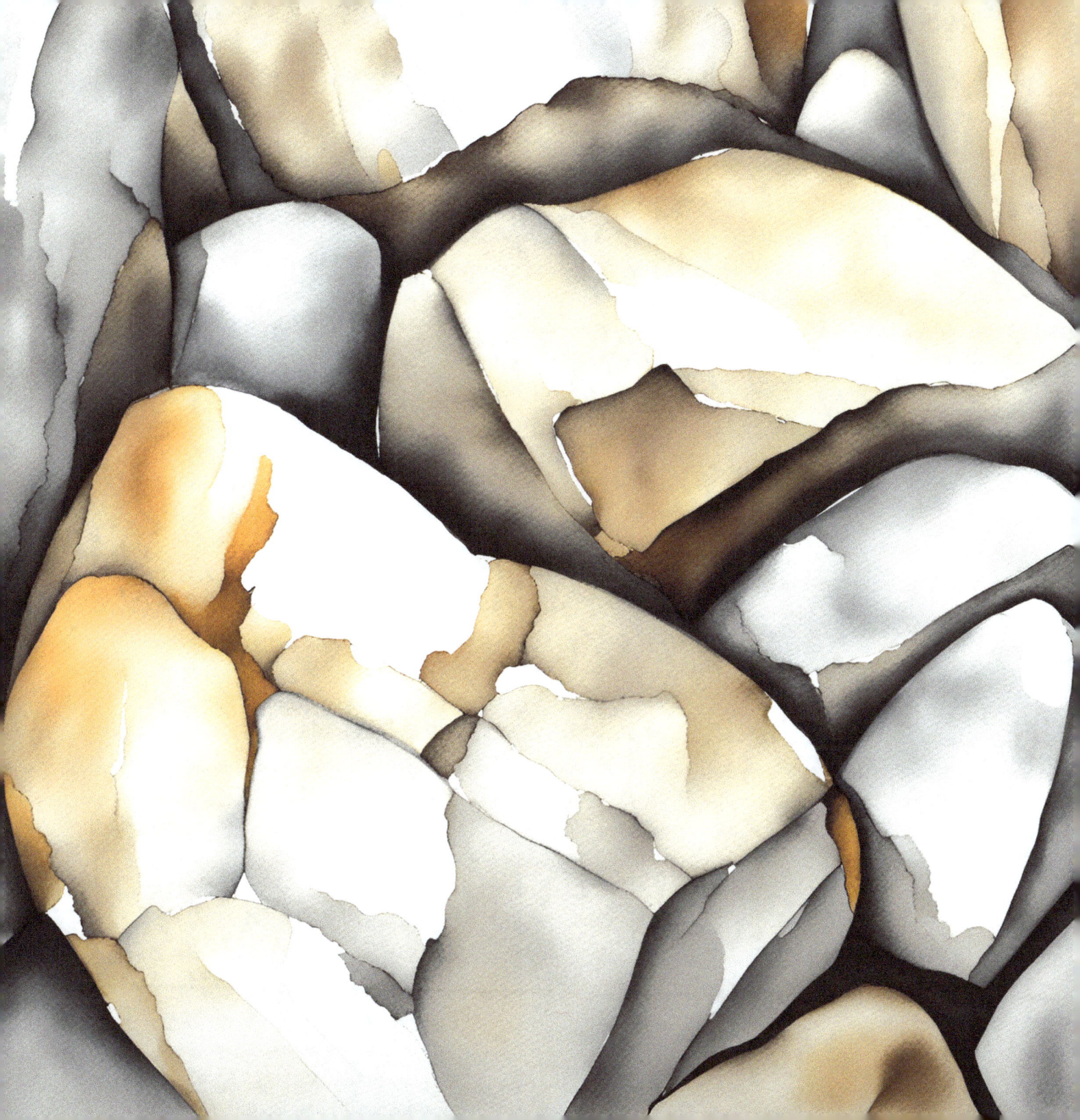

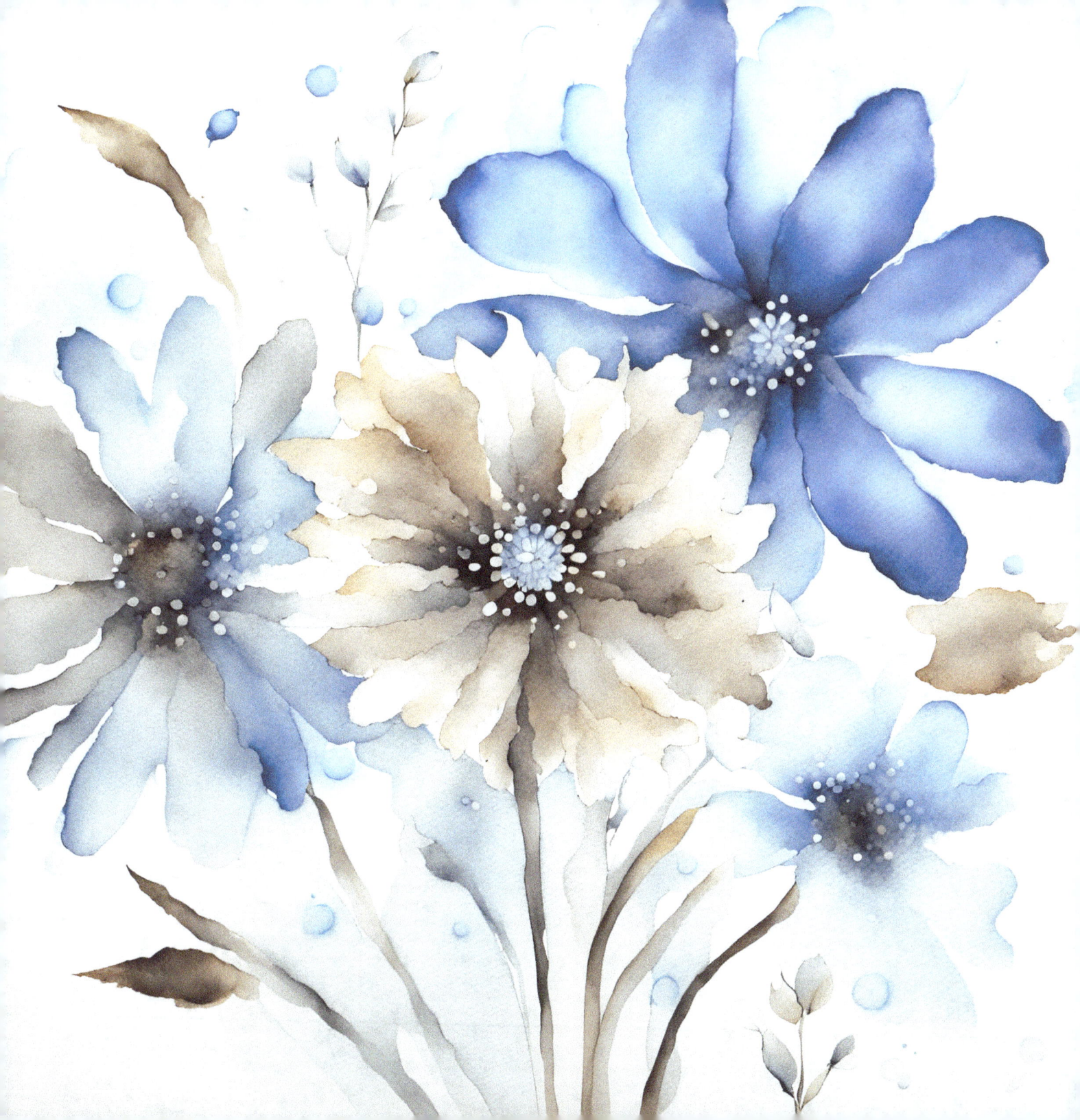

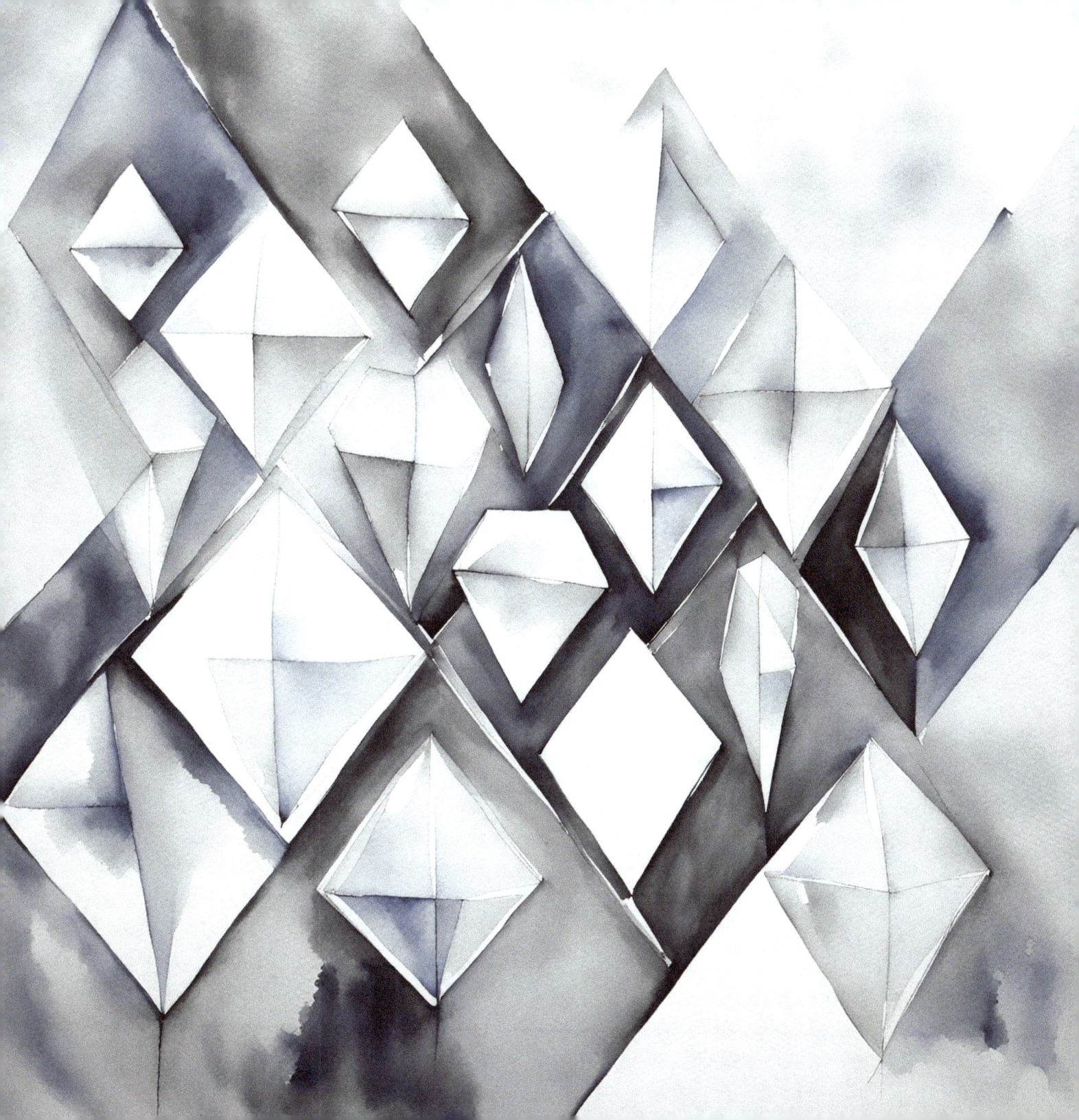

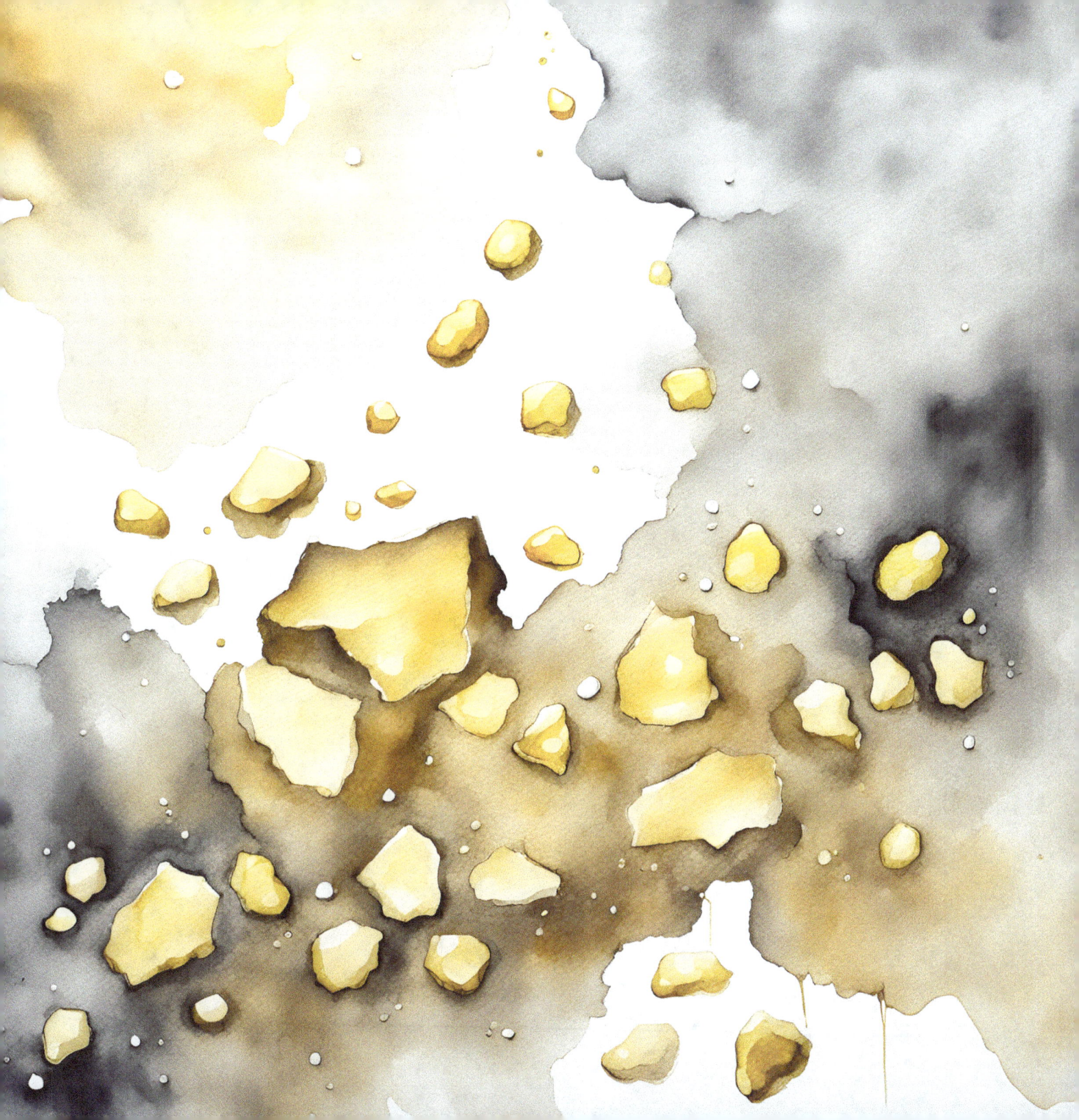

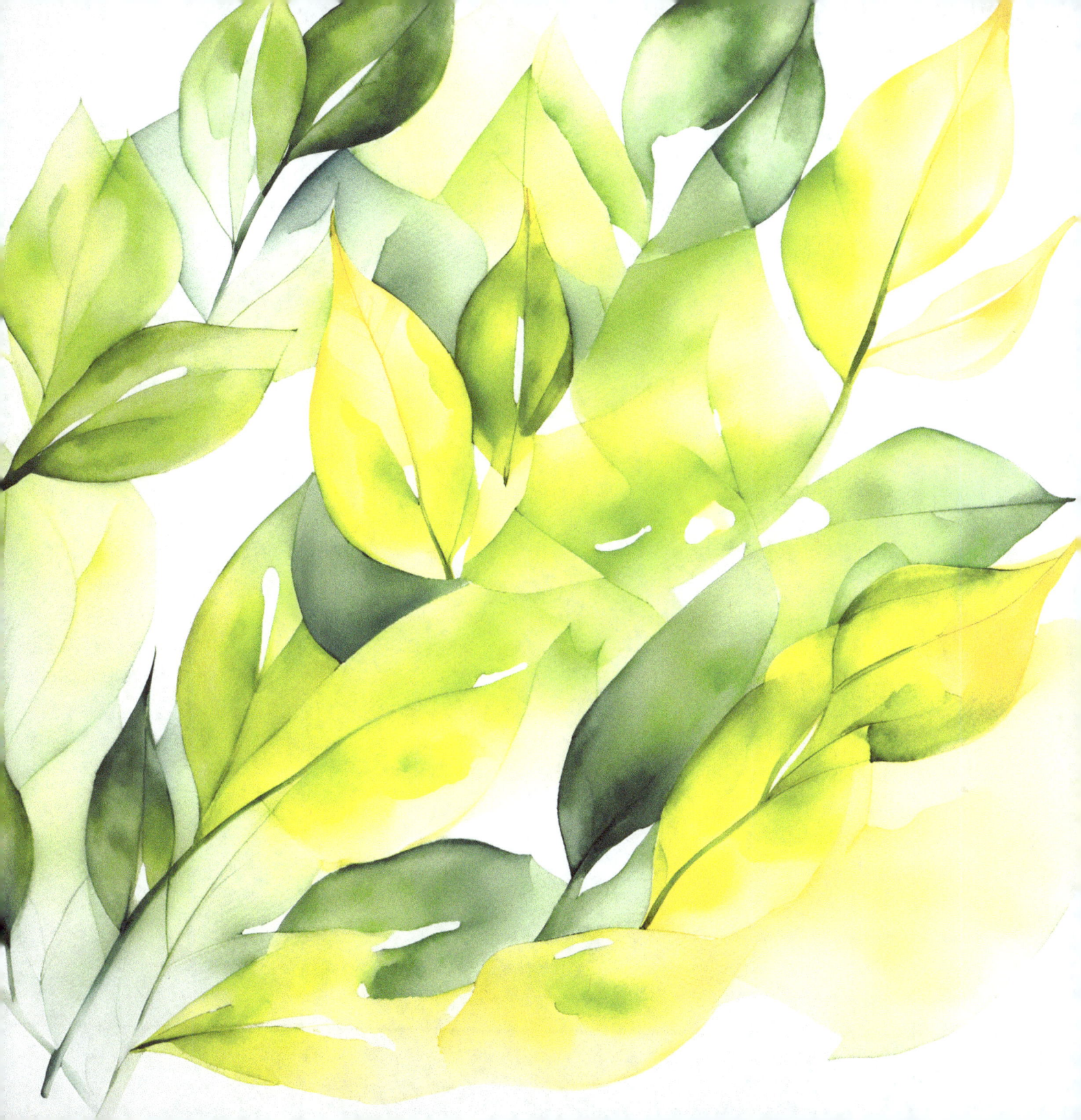

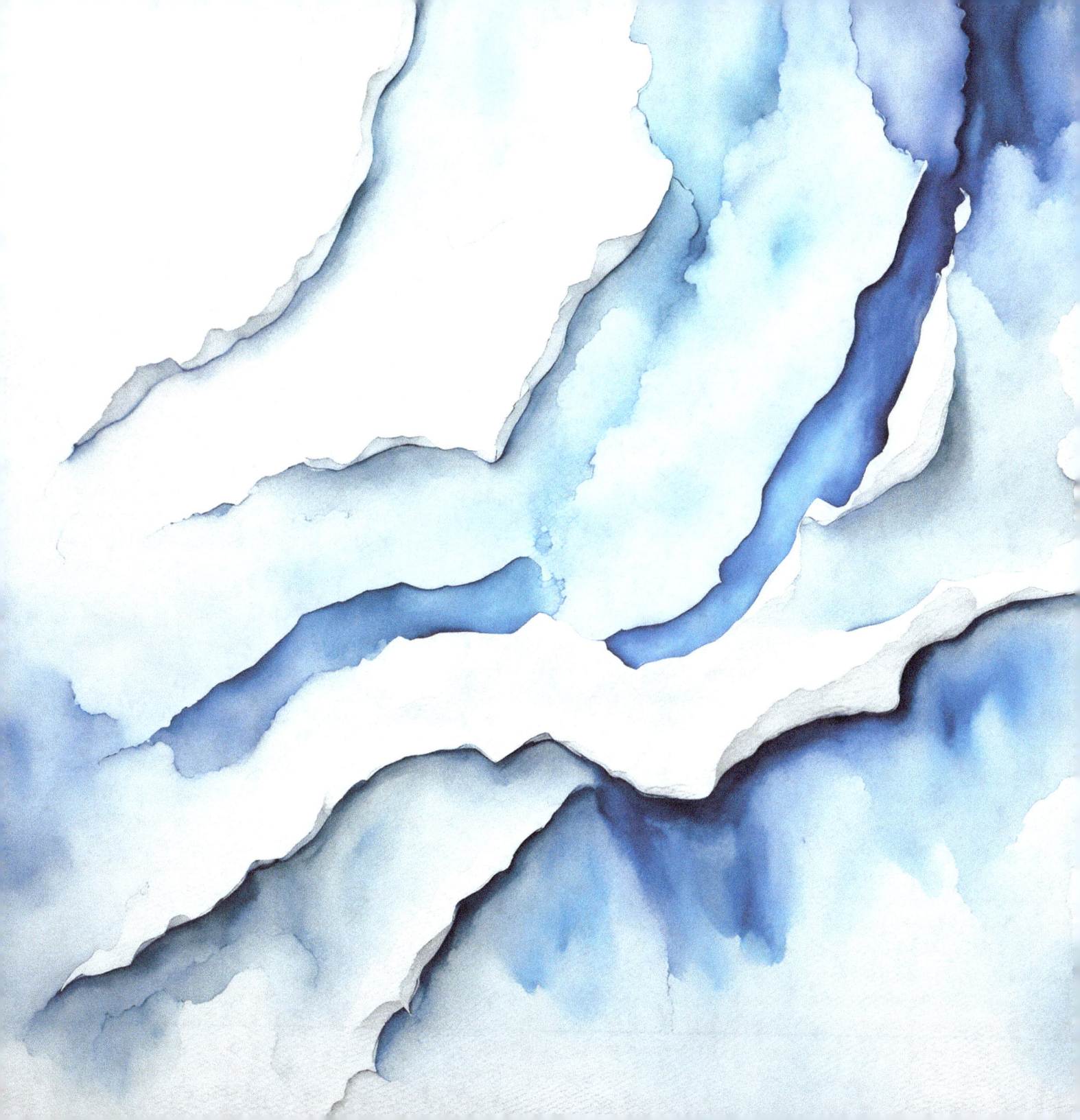

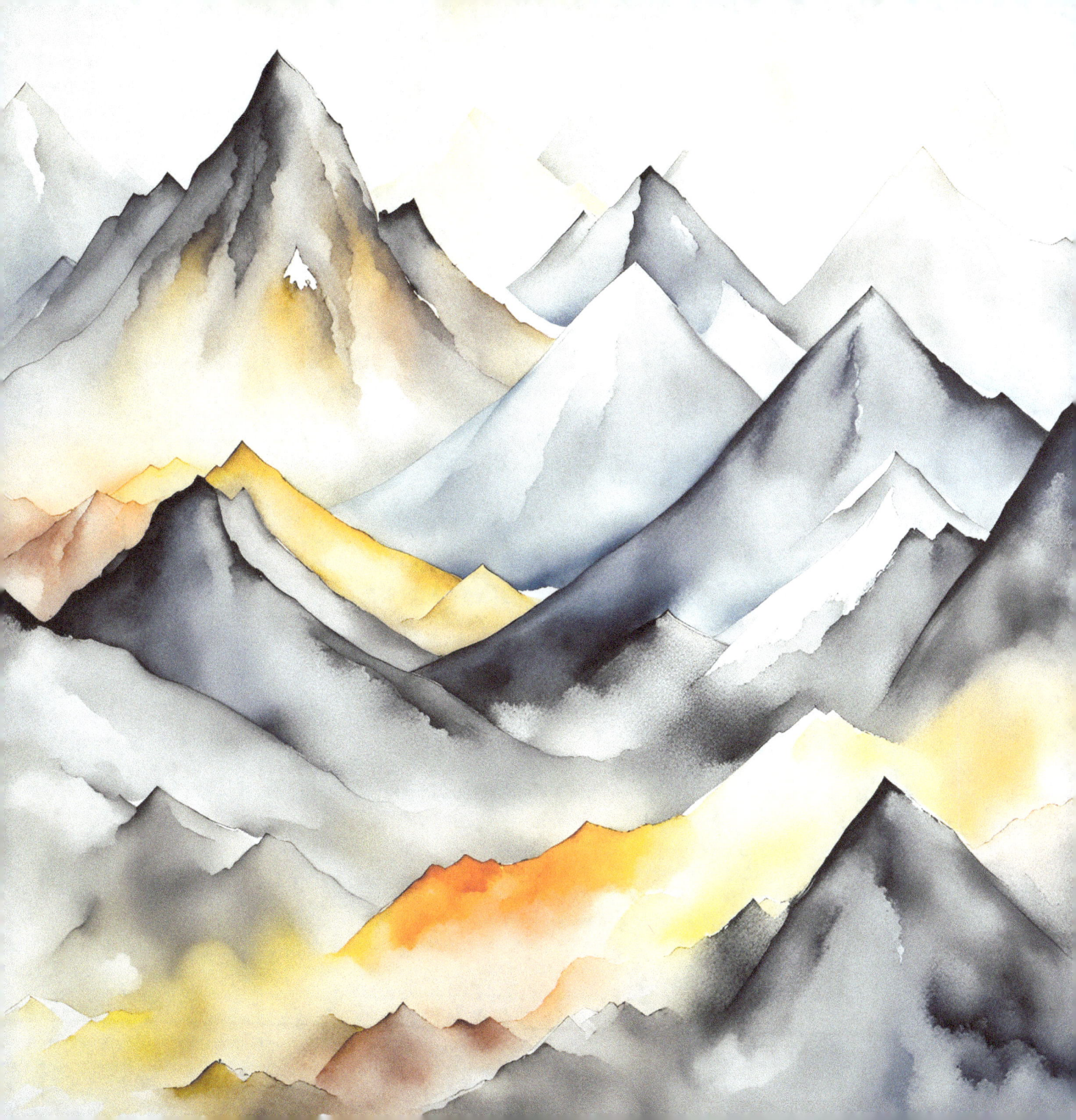

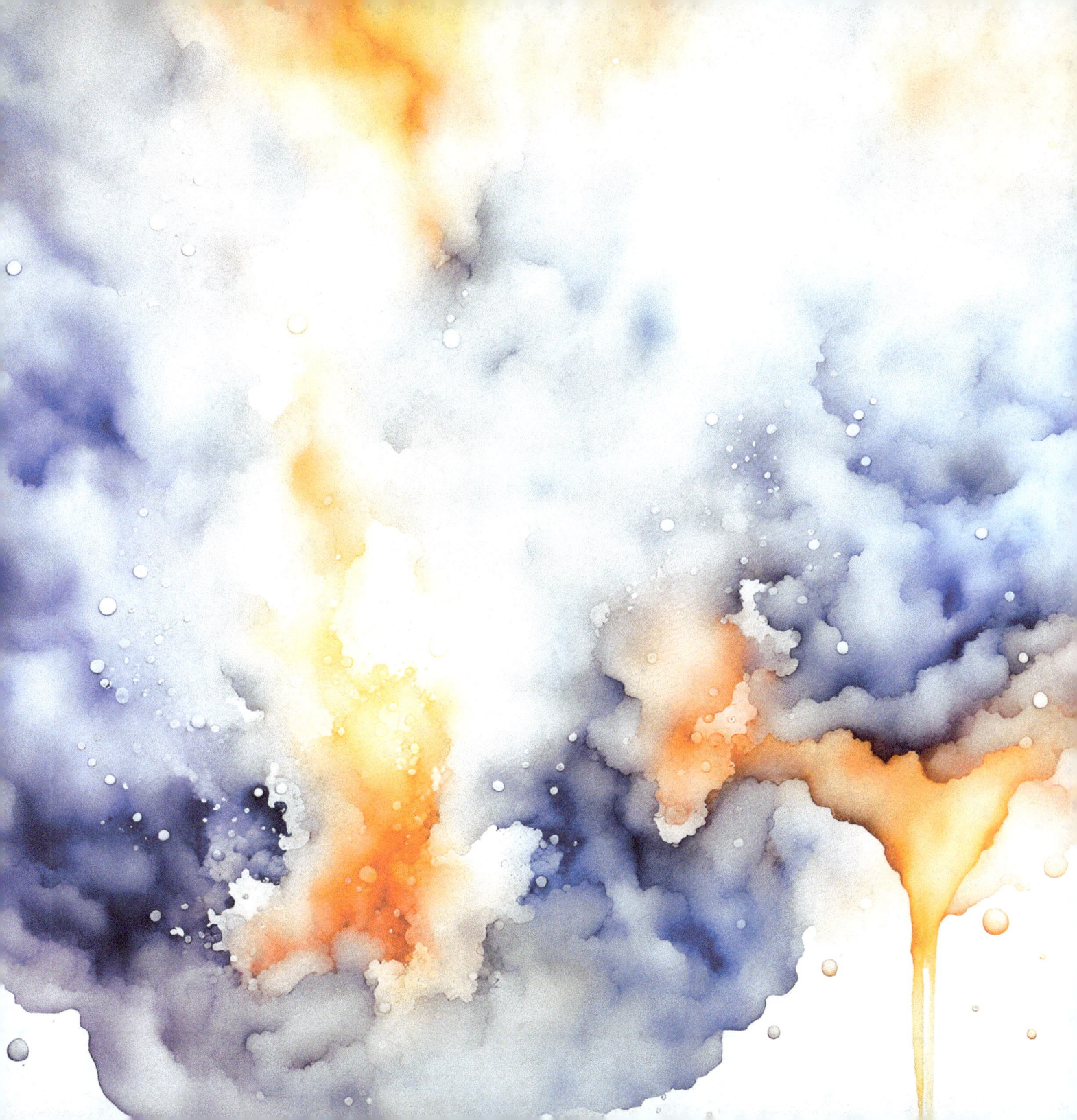

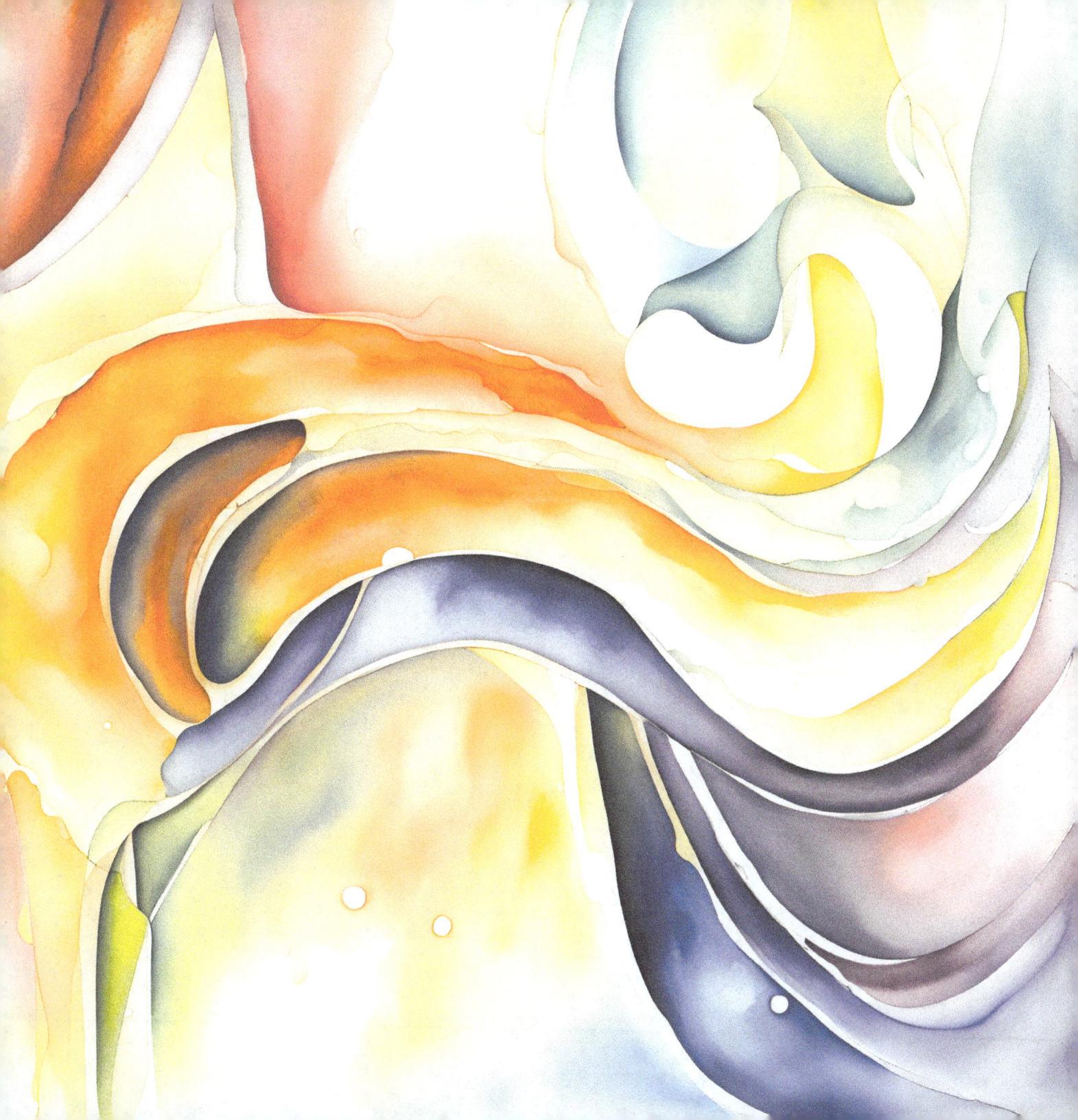

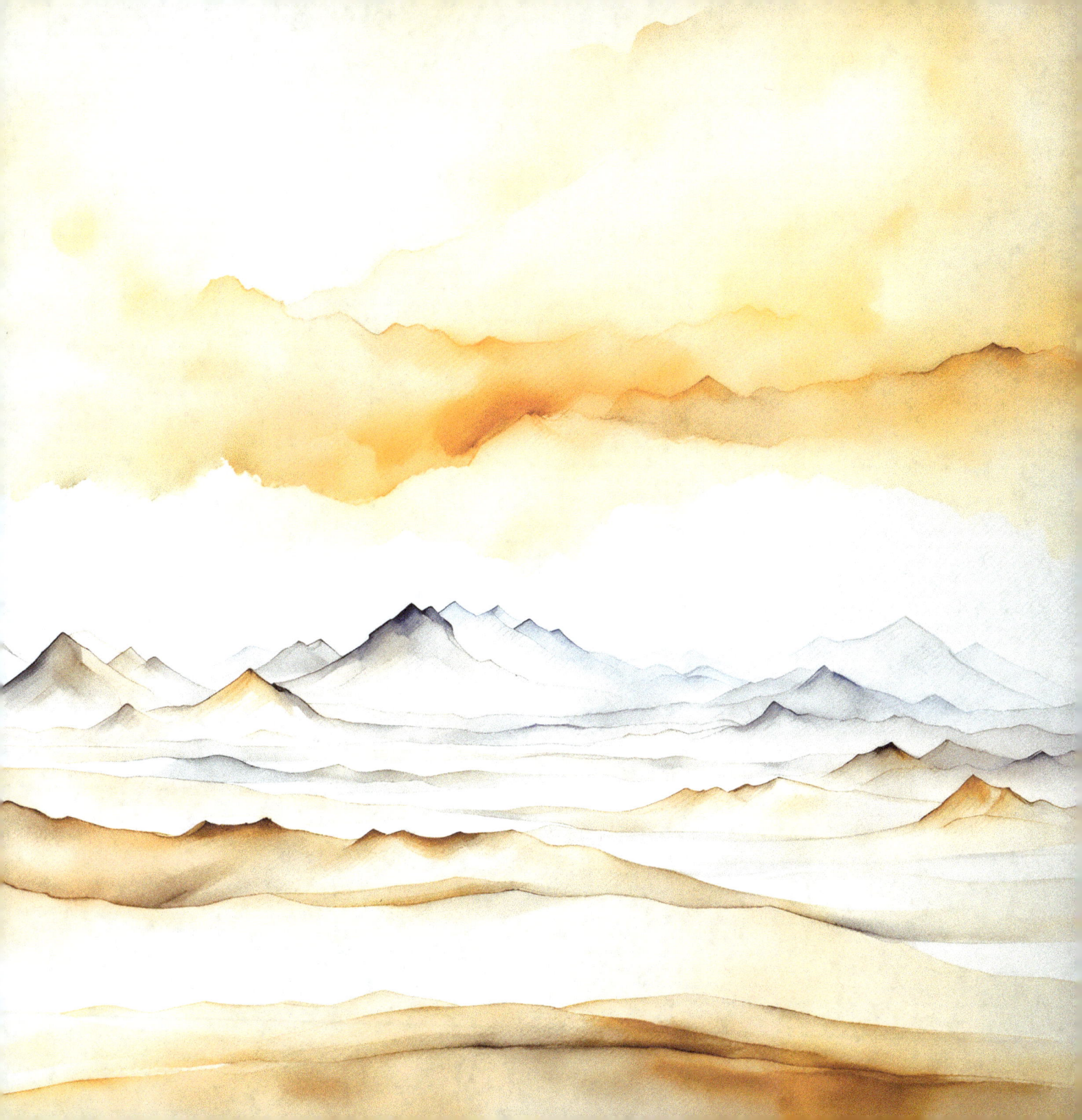

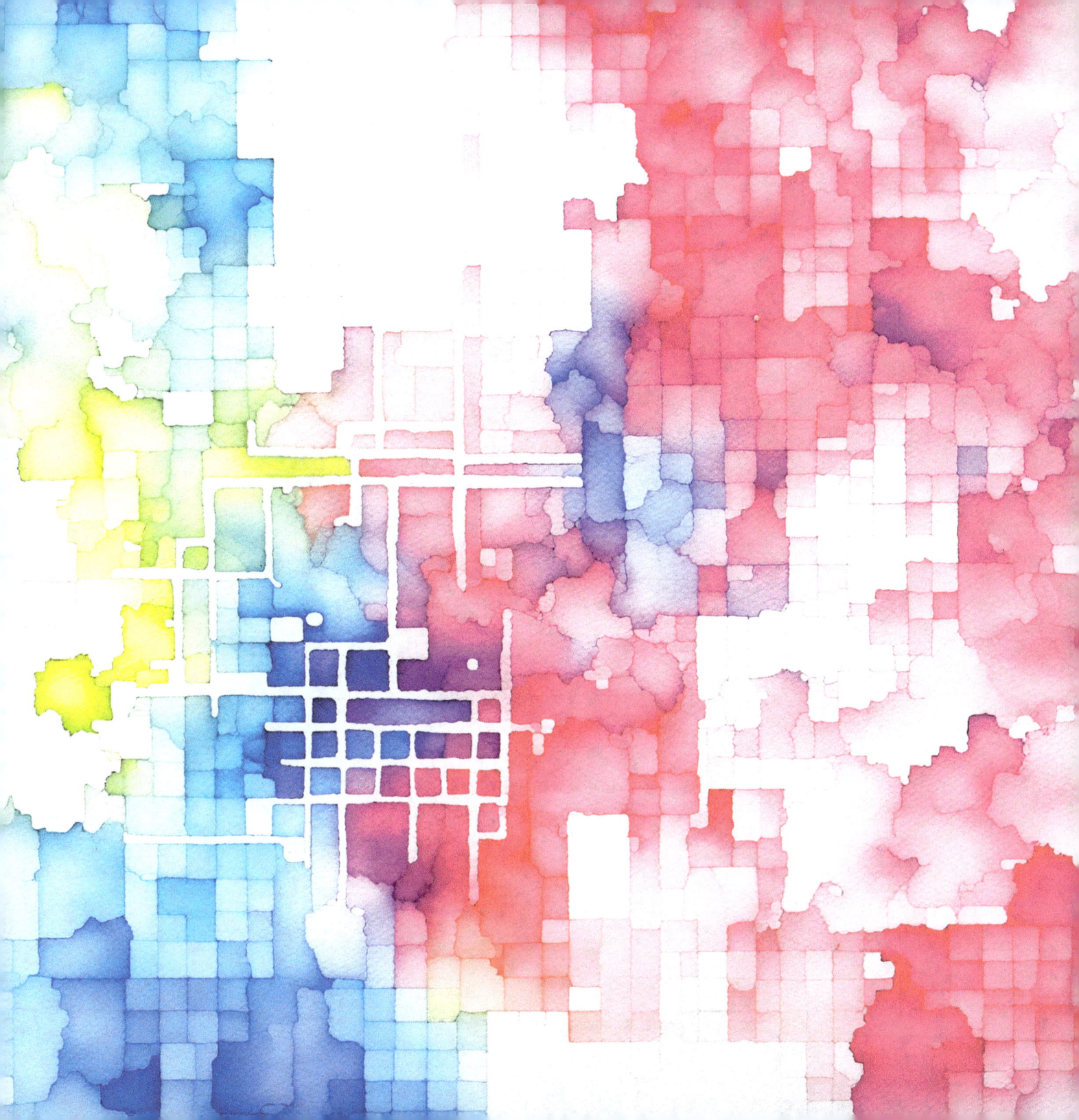

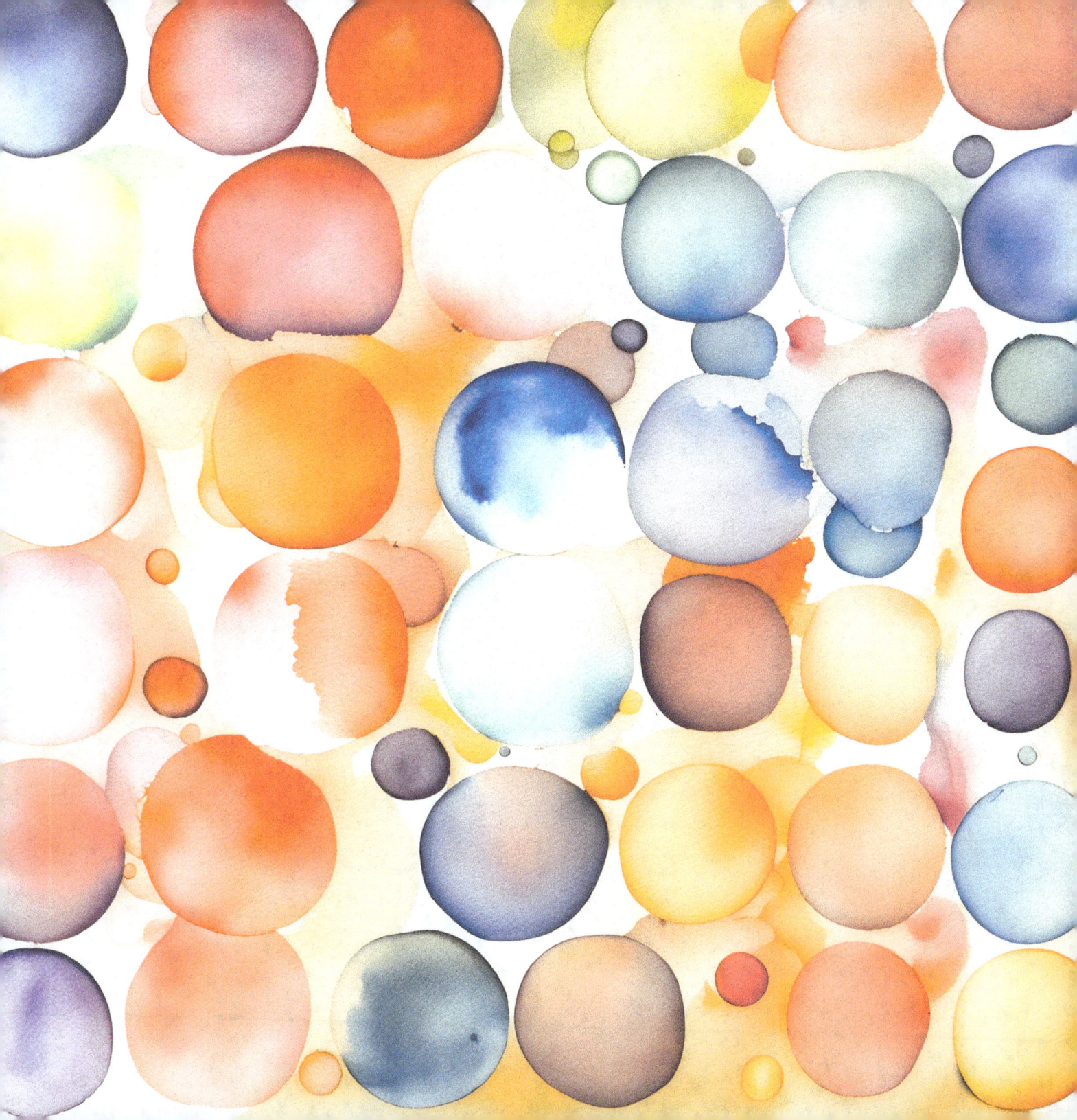

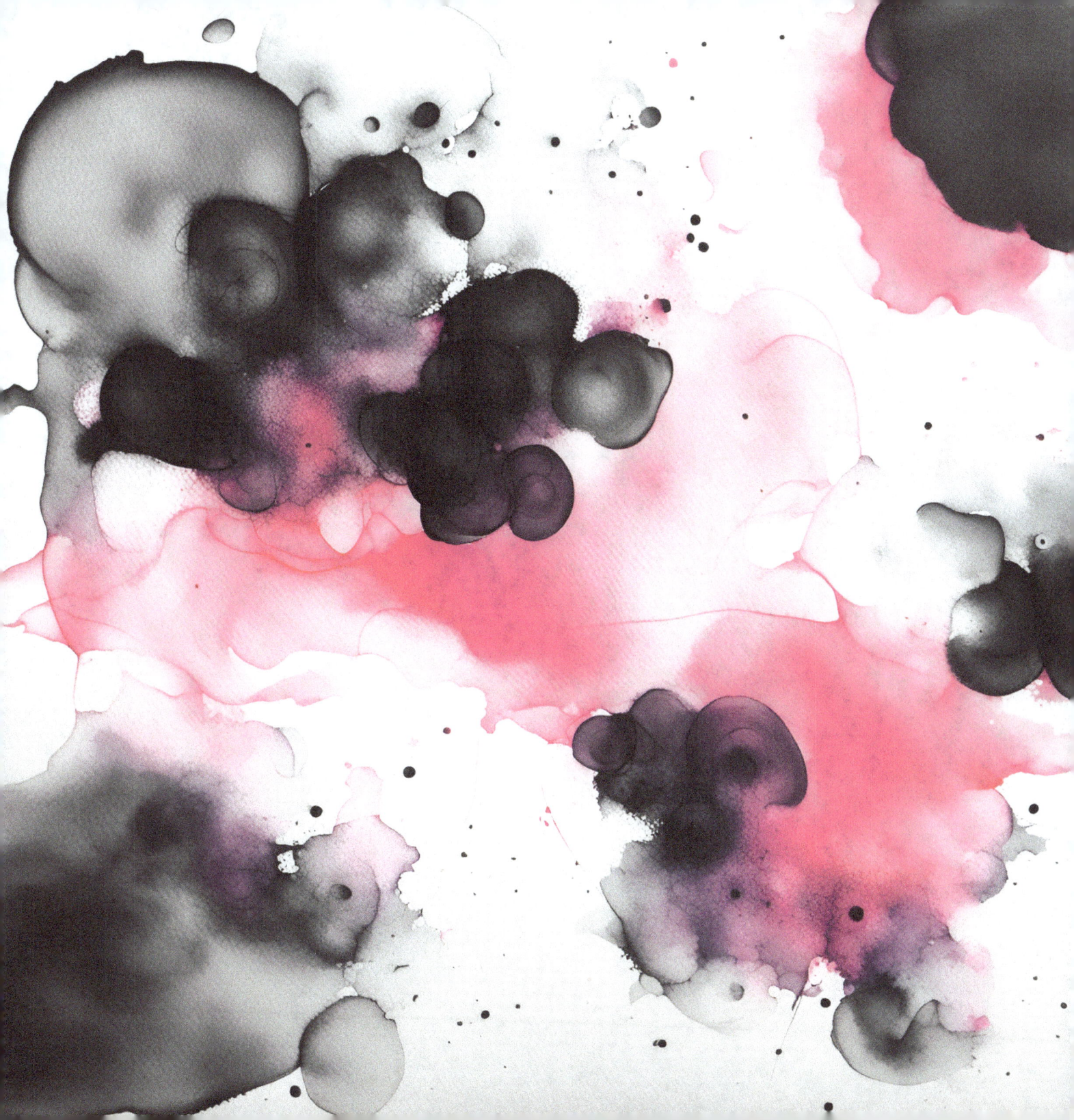

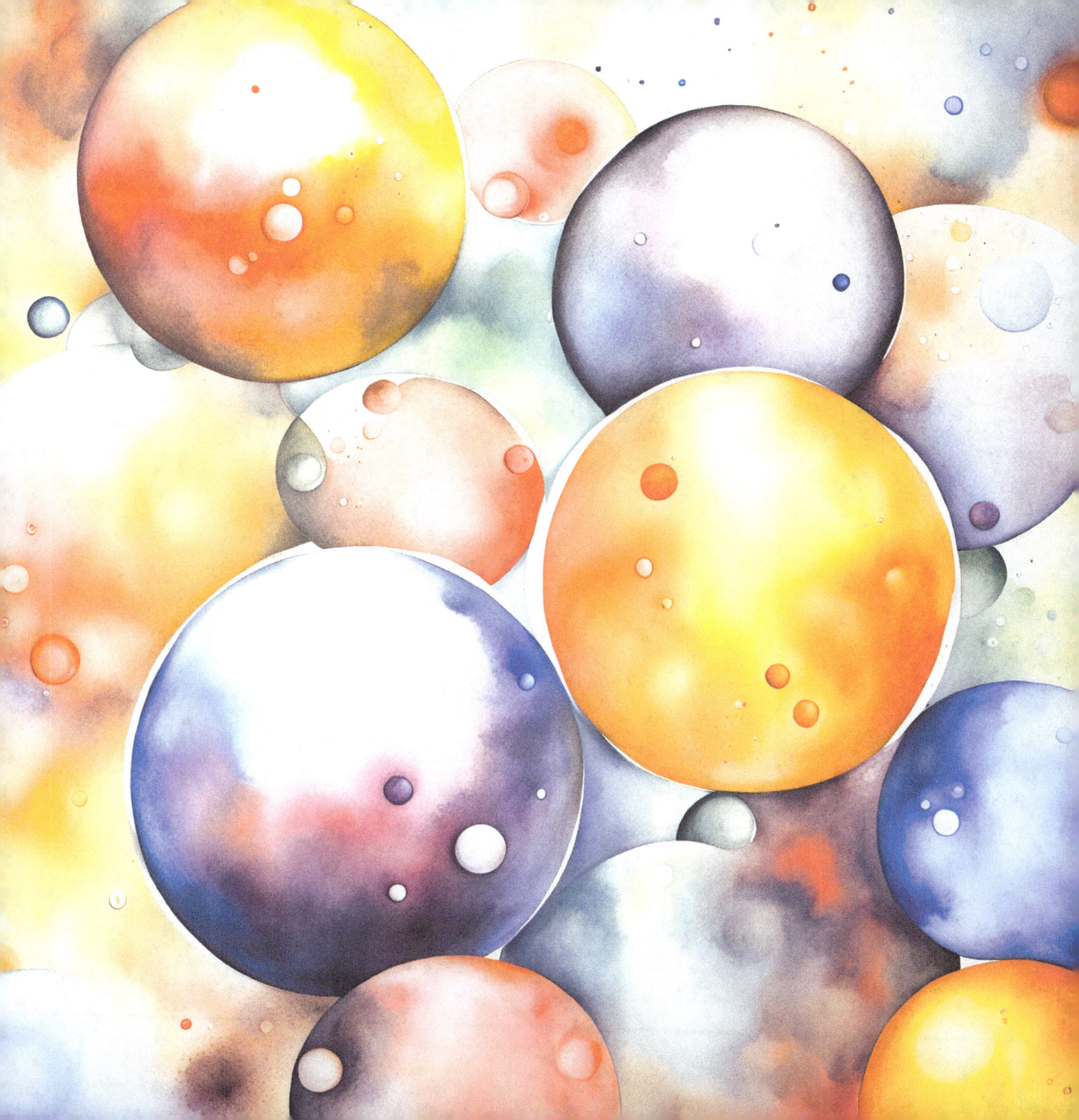

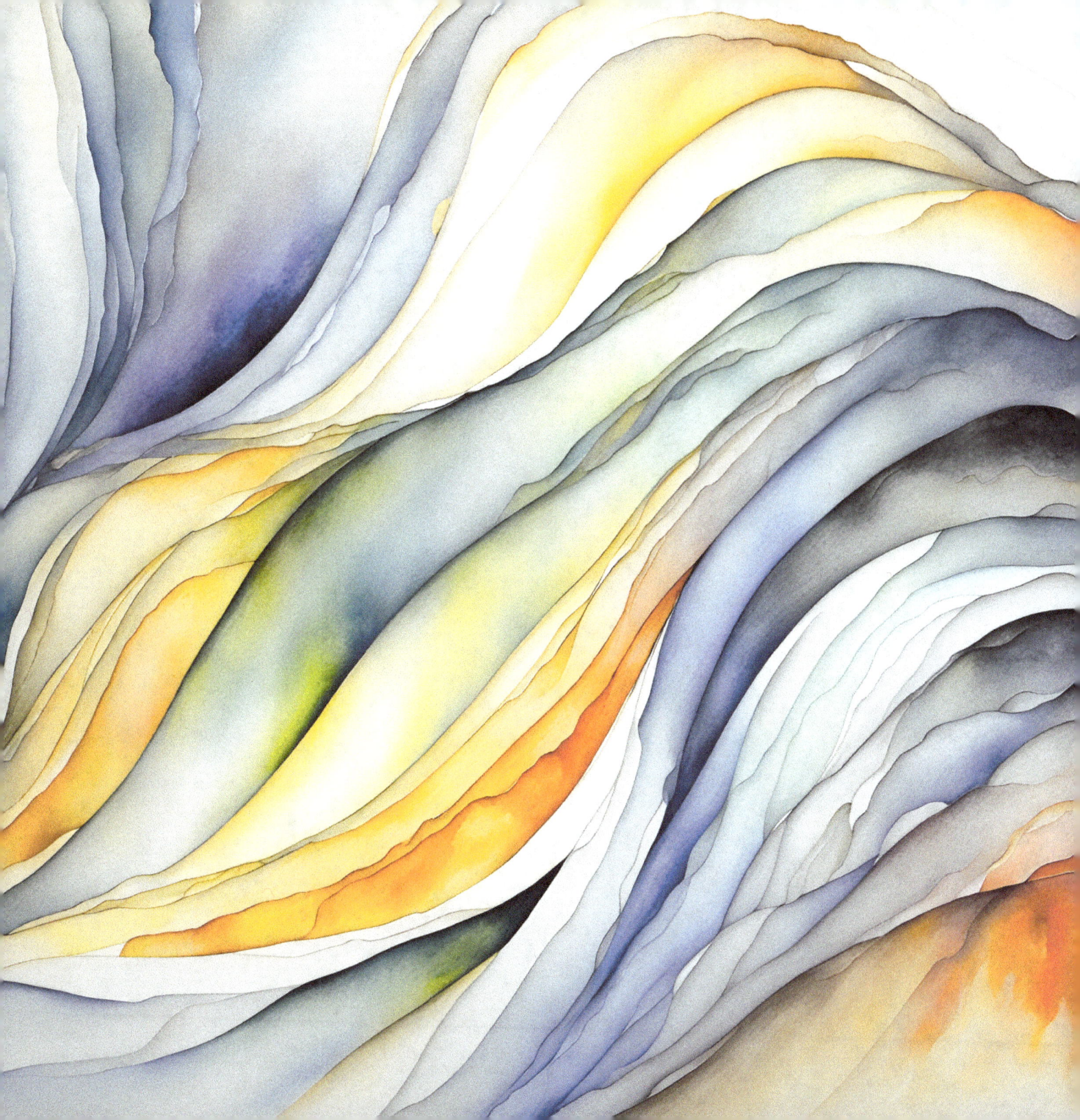

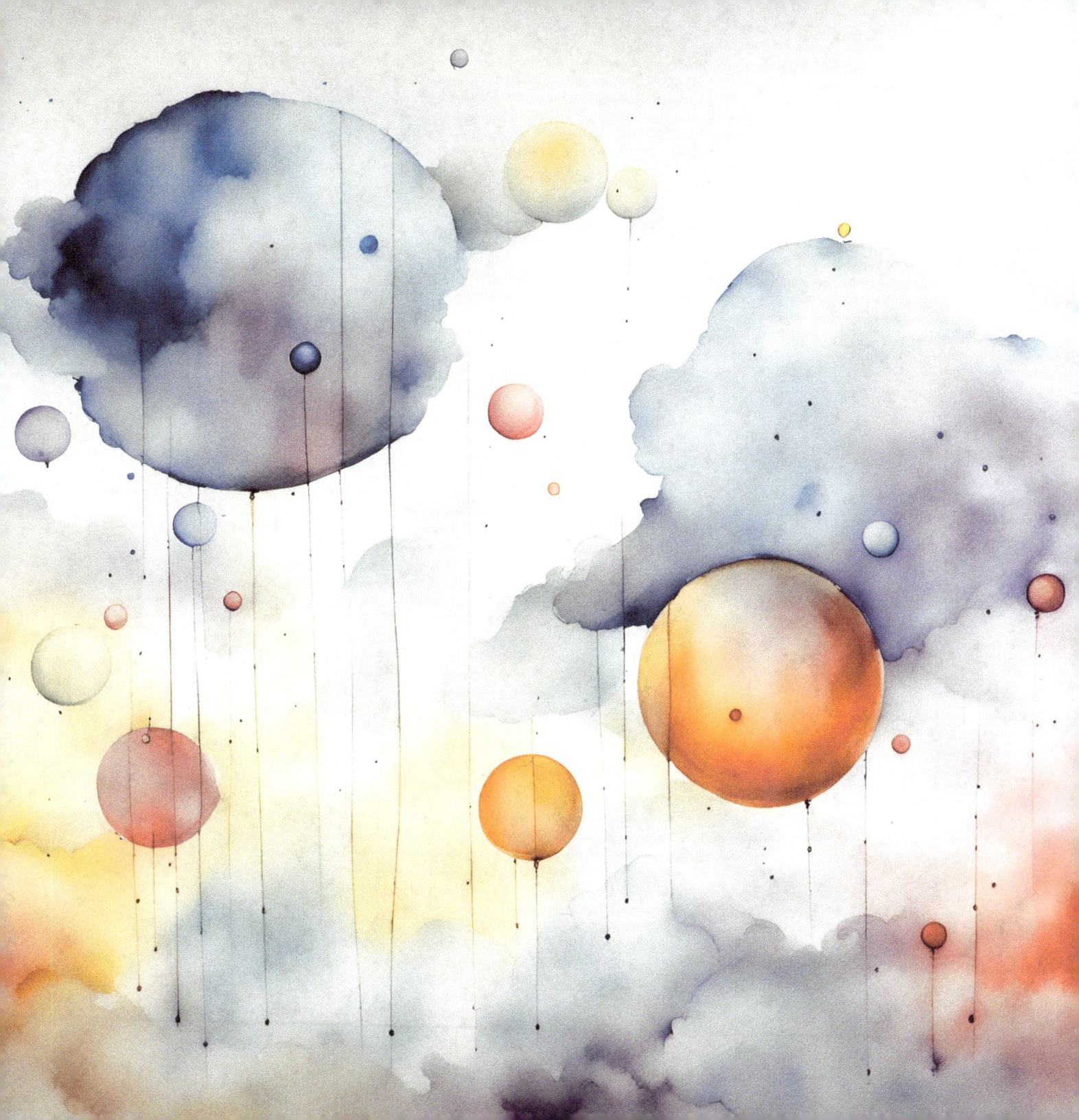

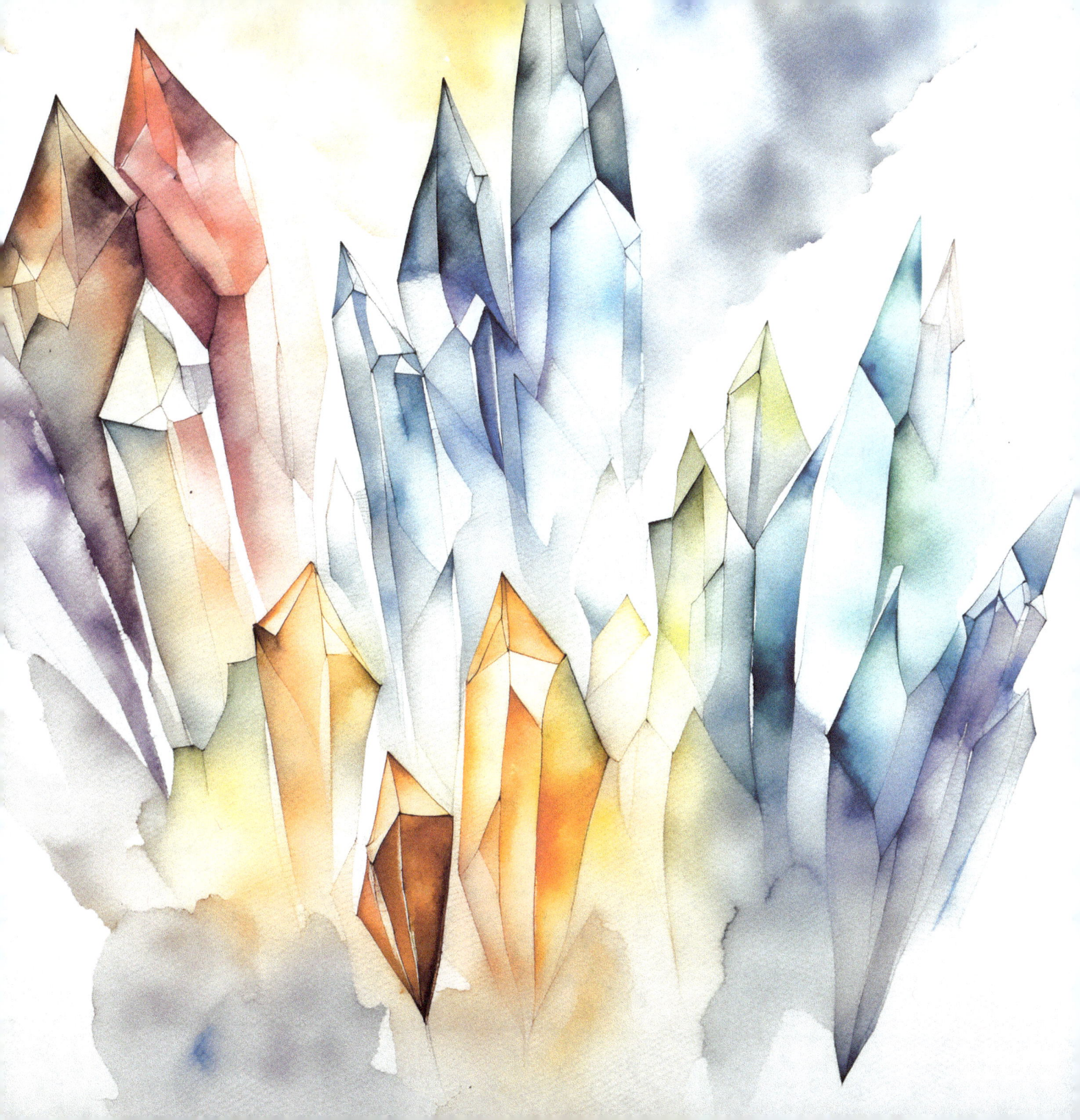

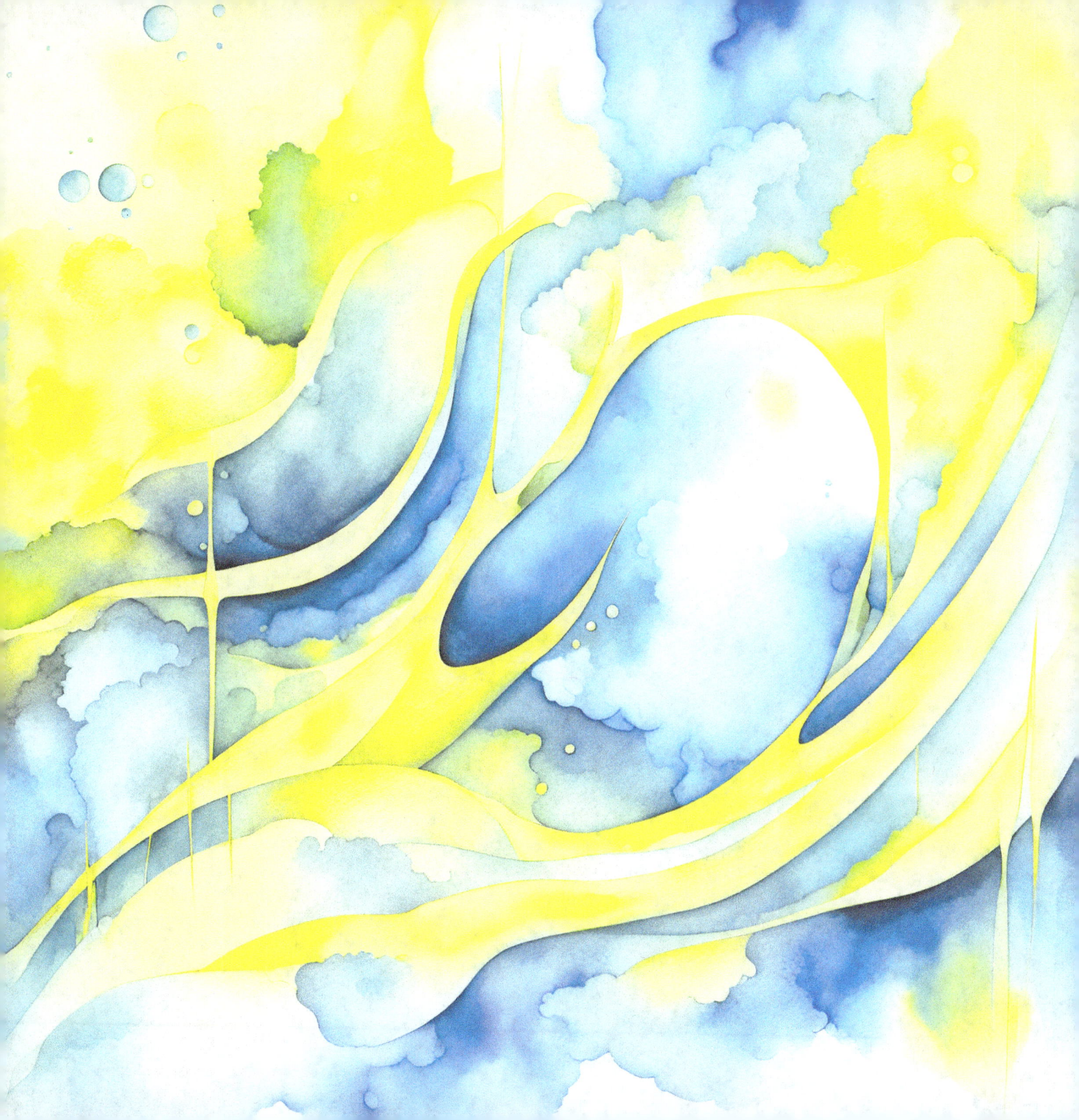

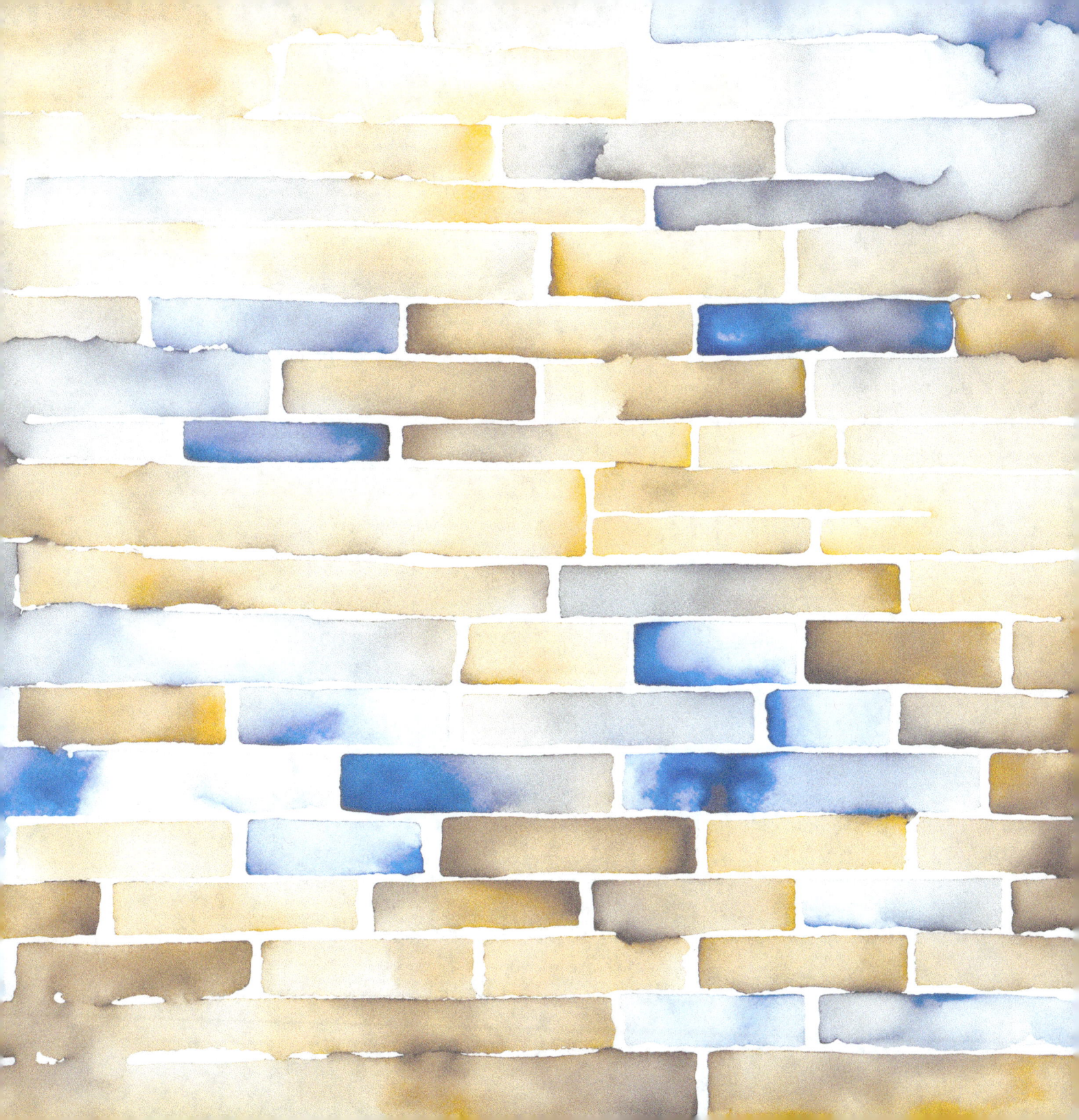

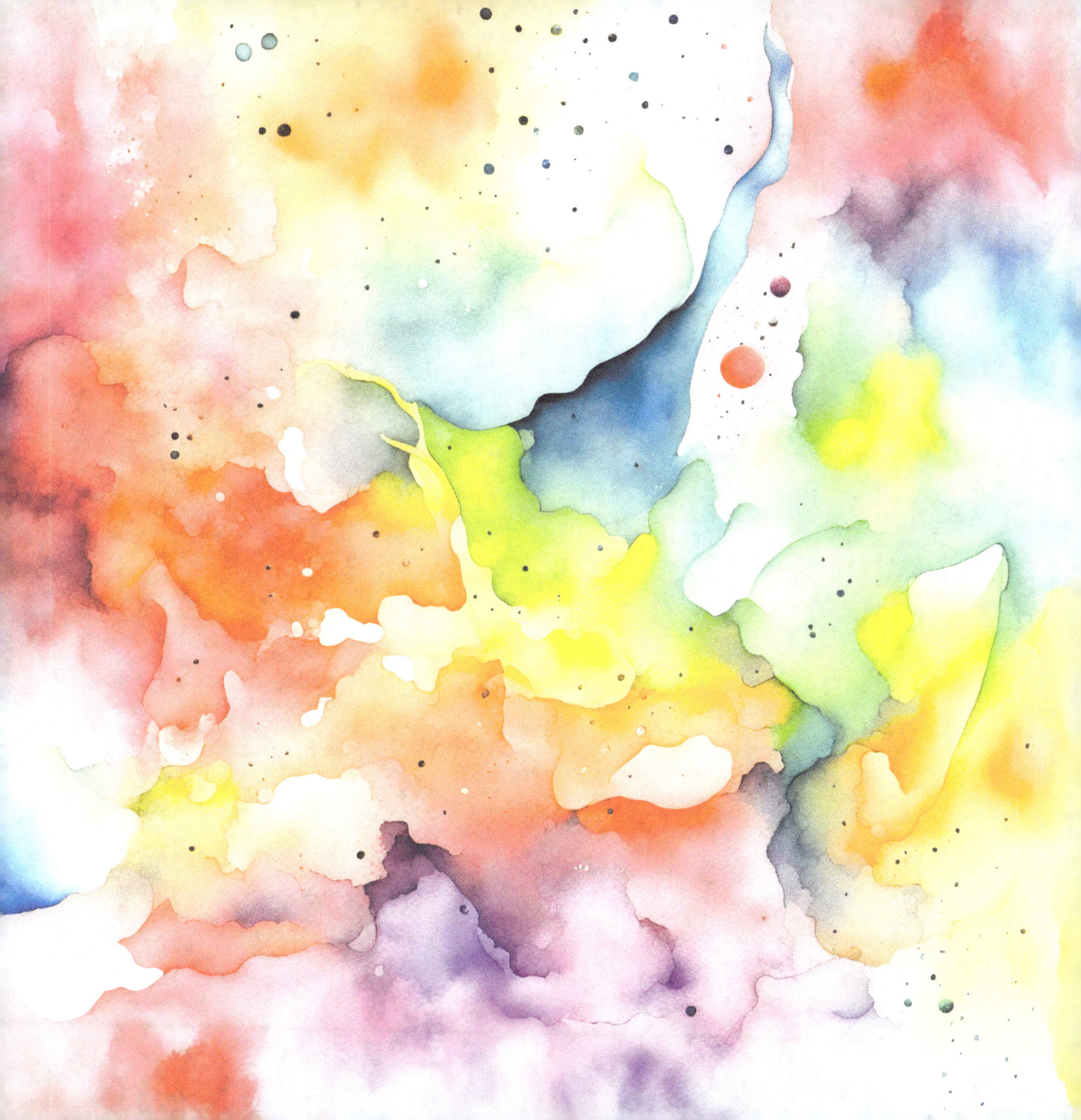

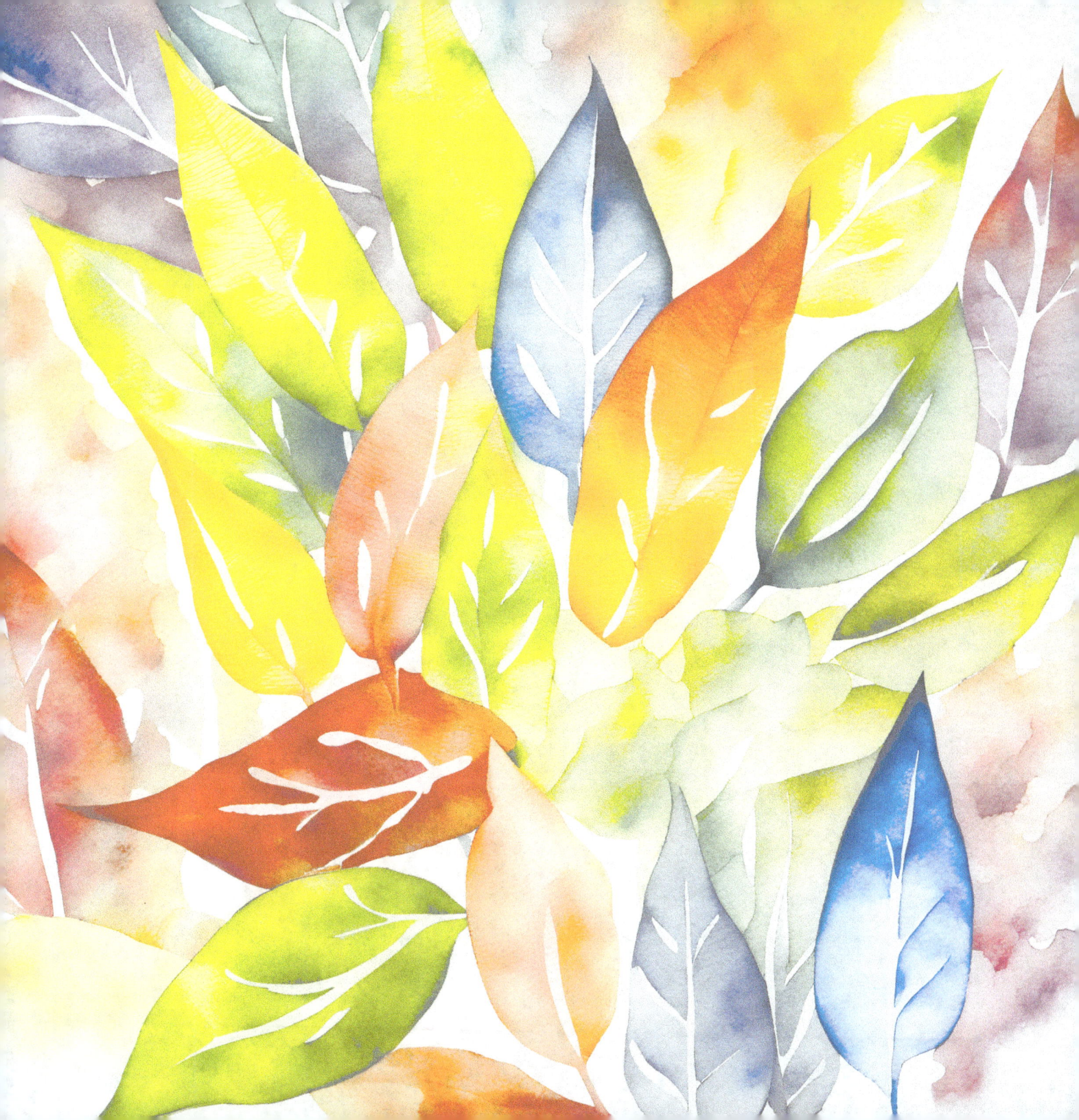

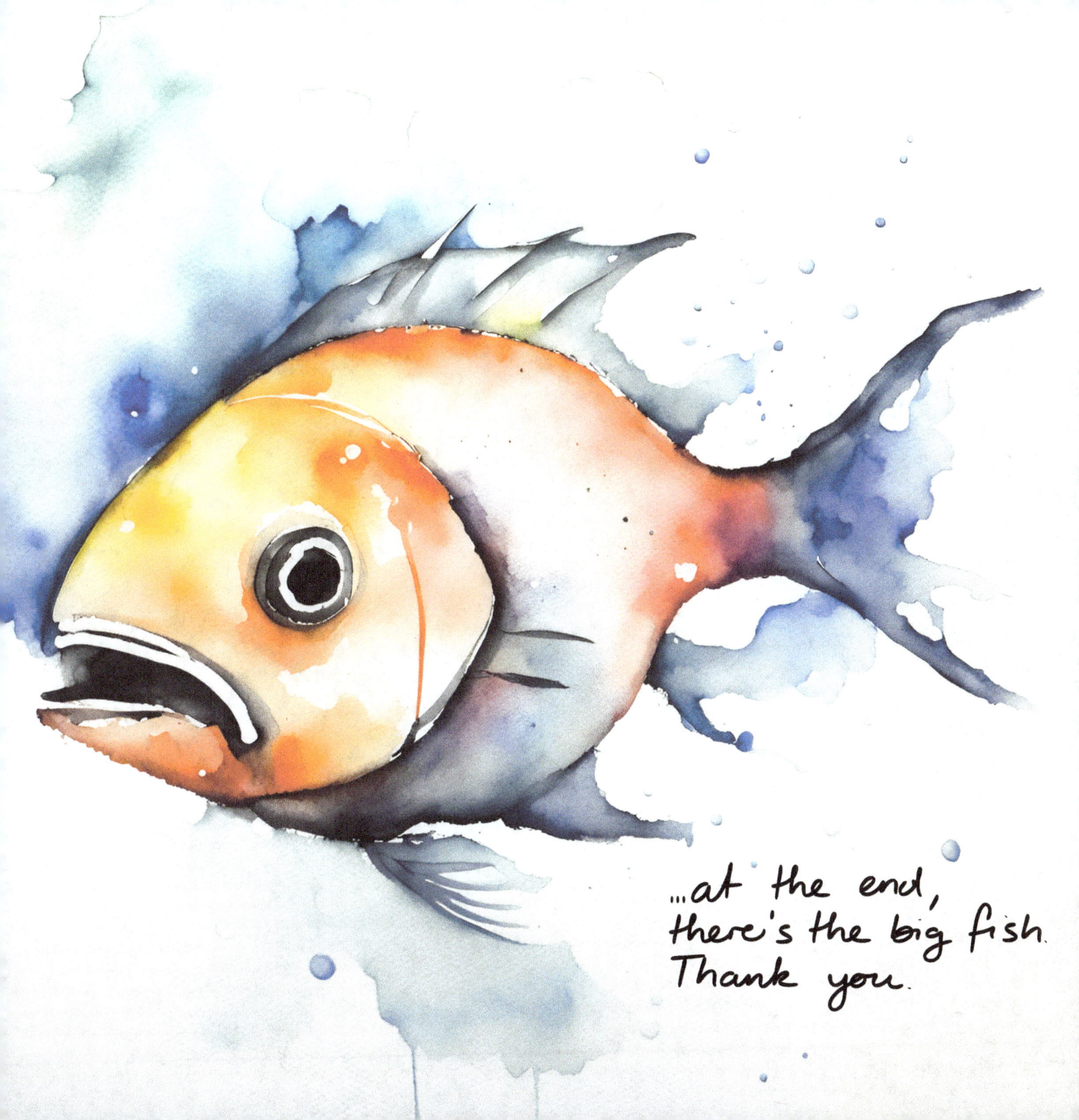

...at the end,
there's the big fish.
Thank you.